Motorcycle Journeys Through

Texas and Northern Mexico

by Neal and Sandy Davis

Whitehorse Press
Center Conway, New Hampshire

Except where noted, photographs were taken by the
author.

We recognize that some words, model names and
designations mentioned herein are the property of
the trademark holder. We use them for
identification purposes only.

Whitehorse Press books are also available at
discounts in bulk quantity for sales and
promotional use. For details about special sales or
for a catalog of motorcycling books and videos,
write to the publisher:
  Whitehorse Press
  107 East Conway Road
  Center Conway, New Hampshire 03813-4012
  Phone: 603-356-6556 or 800-531-1133
  E-mail: CustomerService@WhitehorsePress.com
  Internet: www.WhitehorsePress.com

ISBN-13: 978-1-884313-78-3
ISBN-10: 1-884313-78-7

-   5 4 3 2 1

Printed in China

Acknowledgments

Putting this book together has been a group effort, not just the work of one individual. Contributions come from a multitude of people and resources. Thanks, as always, should be given to the staff of Whitehorse Press for their encouragement and prodding. Dealerships are chock full of folks with local information who were patiently willing to answer my seemingly endless questions. Fellow riders are a wealth of information as you already know. But a very special thanks is due to my wife, Sandy, for her research assistance, initial editing, and adding a female viewpoint not available in my previous efforts—not to mention tagging along and putting up with me.

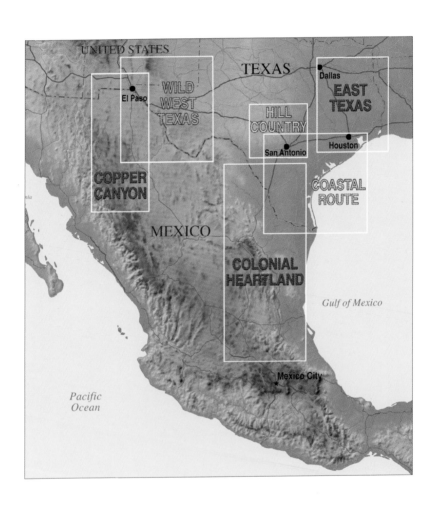

Contents

Foreword

Welcome to *Motorcycle Journeys Through Texas and Northern Mexico,* which is an update of my previous book, *Motorcycle Journeys Through Texas* combined with two additional seven-day routes into and out of Mexico to destinations originally contained in my *Motorcycle Journeys Through Northern Mexico.* I have attempted to update all essential information regarding places to stay, eating establishments, and sights to see. New with this book are some recommendations made by my wife, Sandy. This female influence will be especially appreciated as you snuggle between those clean sheets after having enjoyed a tasty dinner instead of the more basic lodging and eateries included in the previous editions. To you husbands: Beware of any recommendation noted as *Sandy's Choice* unless you have been a bad boy—then they should be seriously considered.

Of special note is the updated information regarding border crossing procedures into and out of Mexico. Also, the helpful contact information contained in the appendix has been completely reviewed and updated.

The only changes from the previous books in roads and routes were those made to avoid difficulties posed by new construction or to add a newly discovered exciting road.

With the combining of rides from two books, some streamlining of the contents was inevitable but this has allowed the inclusion of additional information and resources for those who wish to educate themselves prior to swinging into the saddle. A little time spent learning about these delightful cultures before venturing forth, it will make your trip so much more enjoyable.

Use this book just as a start to your explorations. It would be a shame for example, to limit your riding in the Texas Hill Country to just the routes included herein. I suggest you stop, talk to the locals, fill in the blanks, get lost and enjoy the trip, not just the destination. Mexico offers so much more than could be included here. If you like what you experience from this book, you might try my *Motorcycle Journeys Through Southern Mexico* written a few years back to introduce you to even more fun riding and experiences South of the Border.

Whatever your reason or passion, I hope you find this book to be useful in making your next trip to this area more enjoyable.

Introduction to Texas

Everyone "knows" that Texas is just a huge, flat state. As one uninitiated friend said, "Texas is just a place to get across." While it is true that the vastness of Texas includes long, boring stretches; it also contains some of the best motorcycling roads in the world. Sure Texas is flat—if you leave out the almost 100 mountains that exceed 5,000 feet in altitude. Eight of which exceed 8,000 feet and God only knows how many sub-5,000-foot peaks. Sure, Texas is dry—if you exclude the more than three million acres of inland lakes and rivers, its 600 miles of oceanfront, and the countless bayous and swamps that cover the eastern part of the state. Sure, Texas has no trees—if you wish to ignore more than 20 million acres of woodlands and the Big Thicket. The purpose of this book is to introduce you to these areas with

There is an almost endless variety of roads to explore by motorcycle in Texas. And riders do enjoy the Texas weather.

Just How Big is Texas?

Everyone knows Texas is big. But how can we put this size in perspective? The following facts may help:

1) With a land area in excess of 267,000 square miles, Texas makes up more than seven percent of the entire land mass of the United States. At its widest points, Texas is 801 miles from north to south and 773 miles from east to west. When it was accepted into the Union, Texas was given the option of subdividing into five smaller states.

2) Texas is larger than any European country, and larger than Germany, the United Kingdom, Ireland, Belgium, and the Netherlands *combined*.

3) Texas is larger than all the New England states, New York, Pennsylvania, Ohio and Illinois *combined*. Forty-one counties in Texas are each larger than the state of Rhode Island.

4) If you stand in the city of Orange on the east, you are closer to the Atlantic port of Savannah, Georgia, than you are to El Paso in the west. Of course you have to cross the states of Louisiana, Mississippi, Alabama, and Georgia to reach the Atlantic Ocean.

5) When standing in El Paso you are nearer to Los Angeles than to Orange. Of course, you must pass through the states of New Mexico, Arizona, and California to reach the Pacific Ocean.

6) When you are in Brownsville in south Texas, you are closer to Mexico City than you are to the northern border of Texas and Oklahoma.

7) Standing at the northern border of Texas with Oklahoma, you can almost reach Canada before Brownsville in the south.

8) The Dallas-Fort Worth airport is larger than Manhattan Island.

✪

rides that are every motorcyclist's dream and to a culture that can be as strange to many as any exotic destination in the world. No matter your preference (touring, sport riding, or dual sport), Texas has the ride for you.

What is your riding preference? Do you want hills and twisties to test your sport-bike skills? If so, ride the Hill Country in central Texas or the piney woods in the east. Or, do you enjoy open spaces, dual-sport opportunities, and clear, starry nights? Then give west Texas a try, an area that includes the Davis and Franklin mountains that give you some up and down opportunities. A visit to the Big Bend National Park will leave you

This is one of the reasons you should really not be on rural roads at night.
(photo by Richard Reynolds/TxDOT)

wondering just how big the world must be. If you enjoy riding along mile after mile of pristine beaches with the ocean in view, check out the Coastal Route. This southern route takes you through some wonderful areas to view wildlife, as well as many sites important in the history of the Republic of Texas. I hope you will ride the area that most appeals to you and return time after time to explore other routes. For those of you who live in Texas and have not explored other parts of the state, I hope this will encourage you to do so.

John Steinbeck wrote, "Texas is a state of mind, Texas is an obsession. Above all, Texas is a nation in every sense of the word." Steinbeck hit the nail on the head! Come on down, ride, and enjoy. Two signs you will see often in Texas: DRIVE FRIENDLY and DON'T MESS WITH TEXAS. Both are good advice.

Information & Cultural Tidbits

Each chapter in this book is based at a major city with good air transportation services. You can ship your bike to that city, fly in, and be on your way, or you can arrange to rent a motorcycle when you arrive. The Appendix lists information to help you with either of these as well as recommended motorcycle dealerships.

This book does not attempt to provide detailed sightseeing options in the major cities, because this book focuses on riding the open road. However, if you wish to spend a day or two exploring El Paso, San Antonio, Dallas, or Houston, there are many good guidebooks which cover the local sights. Call the local visitors center or Chamber of Commerce or visit their web sites to obtain up-to-date information. By spending some time exploring the major cities, you will get a better overall feeling and understanding for the variety of lifestyles in Texas. A quick overview of options in each city of interest to motorcyclists is included at the beginning of each chapter. In the route descriptions I have tried to point out interesting stops, side trips, eating places, and motorcycling hangouts that will be worth a try.

AVERAGE DAY

How many miles make for a good day's ride? This varies widely with the rider and his or her style and habits. Think of days in hours instead of miles; the days in this book vary from less than one hundred miles (a lot of traffic and sightseeing) to almost four hundred (across wide open spaces of west Texas). The daily routes are planned so that your actual time from leaving your motel or campsite in the morning to arriving at your evening's destination will be eight to ten hours, including time for a short break mid-morning and mid-afternoon, a reasonable lunch stop, and occasional time off the bike to stretch your legs and enjoy the roadside sights. Consider your own riding habits and adjust your plans as needed. Also, please consider all mileages given in this book as approximate. Motorcycle odometers vary greatly and yours may not be the same as the one used to measure the routes for this book.

NAVIGATION

The daily routes suggested in this book are often not direct routes from Point A to Point B. They try to get you onto the small backroads that are more enjoyable rides. As a result of this, you will encounter some turns

Barbeque cook-offs are big events throughout Texas, with lots of ego and pride at stake. (photo by Michael A. Murphy/TxDOT)

where the signs indicate your next destination is in another direction. Follow the directions in the text, and you will eventually get to that destination too—but in a more interesting, fun way.

LODGING

In the major cities you will have the option of hotels and motels in every price range and category. Unless there is a truly unique place to stay, in or near these cities, I don't make a recommendation. You can pick your favorite chain or just "eyeball" a Mom and Pop that looks good (I like the ones with the chairs in front of your door). On the road, the overnight stops listed are clean and generally moderately priced, with good dining facilities nearby. Sometimes you will have no other choice available. On several routes, some options are given for the upscale rider at various ranches and resorts. Of special note are lodgings shown as *Sandy's Choice* which reflect an upscale spot that can be used for that special occasion or as an attempt to recover lost ground with your companion; beware, these are what are known as "budget busters!" This book also suggests camping options, when available.

DINING

Texas offers all the usual fast food outlets in almost every town. I attempt to help you avoid these by pointing out local eateries that reflect the tastes of the area. Not surprisingly, barbecue and Texas chicken-fried steak can be found almost everywhere. Tex-Mex cafés throughout the state offer some of the best food anywhere in the world. The fresh seafood found along the coast is a delight. Certain rural sections of the state have culinary traditions you might not expect—German food in the Hill Country and Cajun cuisine in the east—but you should take advantage of the opportunity to enjoy these local specialties.

ROAD HAZARDS AND DRIVING ETIQUETTE

Because of the heat, you should make sure you have a "foot" of some kind to place under your kickstand. Some people might not believe asphalt can exist in a liquid state—they have never been to Texas during the summer!

Roads in Texas are often resurfaced using the "chip and seal" method, a process whereby liquid asphalt is poured on an existing highway and then loose gravel is layered on top. After a few months, when the traffic has driven the gravel into the asphalt, the remaining gravel is removed. These areas are usually clearly marked by signs indicating loose gravel. Unless you happen upon one of these sections just a few days after the work was completed, they should present no real problem.

On routes that go through open-range country, livestock being in the road is always a possibility. Be alert for cattle guards—short sections of parallel pipes running perpendicular to the road—which are designed to keep livestock from crossing into a new area. Texas also has a healthy deer population, especially in the hill country.

Many rural roads in Texas have broad paved shoulders on each side. When being overtaken by faster traffic, locals commonly maintain their

Relaxing by your tent after a good day's ride is what motorcycle touring is all about.

Just How Hot is a Texas Summer?

There are many sayings about how hot it gets in Texas during the summer. Here are a few:

1) Hot water comes from both taps.

2) The temperature drops below 90 degrees and you start looking for a sweater.

3) One of your biggest fears is that you will drop your bike in a parking lot and cook to death.

4) You realize that asphalt has a liquid state.

5) You coat your tongue with Tabasco sauce to cool your mouth off.

6) You realize the best parking spot is not the one nearest your destination, but where there is shade.   ✪

speed, but pull over to these shoulders—a nice gesture. Don't be shy about passing slower vehicles like this, and return the favor when you are being overtaken.

WHEN TO GO

Texas is hot. During the months of July and August, riding a motorcycle can be less than enjoyable—even dangerous—due to the heat. Be careful to stay hydrated during warmer weather. The winter months can be wonderful, as long as you don't catch one of the few "blue northers" that come through two or three times a year. Fortunately, these cold snaps typically last only for a day or two. The best time to ride in Texas is March through June and October through December. Along the coast and in the Hill Country, riding is a year-round sport.

West Texas is dry, averaging less than eight inches of rain per year. East Texas, however, is quite wet, with up to fifty inches of rain per year (mostly in the summer months in the form of afternoon thundershowers or "frog stranglers").

EVENTS AND RALLIES

If you enjoy attending motorcycle rallies and events, a wonderful free service is available through the people at Texmoto (www.texmoto.com), avid bikers and publishers of *Ride Texas* magazine. Once you have signed up for their free service, you will receive a weekly email listing events for the following month, including dates, locations, and links to the organizers' web sites.

TEXAS CULTURE

Not only is there superb riding in Texas, the culture and personality of the Lone Star State can be as unique and special as any exotic destination in the world. Some of the nation's largest cities are in Texas. Other sections have the lowest population density in the United States. The state was settled over a long period of time and its current inhabitants reflect both the myriad environmental differences and the diverse cultural backgrounds of original settlers.

In east Texas, you will find the French and Cajun influence evident in the architecture, food, pace of life, and speech patterns. Along the border with Mexico, a predominantly Hispanic population commonly uses Spanish for roadside signs and daily interaction. The Hill Country hangs on to the food and language of its Germanic roots; at many area events, German is the most common tongue. West Texas leans heavily on its ranching and cowboy history.

Coming from such varied backgrounds, what binds these people into one called Texan? Texas was settled notably later than most other parts of the United States, by a sturdy stock of pioneers who tended to take risks and be somewhat less likely to bend to convention and authority. The image of

Along most Texas roads, you may encounter strange wildlife at any time.
(photo by Gay Shackelford/TxDOT)

High School Football

Texans have great pride and are fiercely competitive. Nowhere is this more evident than at a high school football game. Not only will the worth and reputation of the school be on the line, but the entire town's as well. It is not unusual for a promising prospect from far across the state to find that his parents are moving to a new job located in a town that just happens to need a player at his position. In larger cities, you will find 20,000-seat stadiums filled on Friday nights with screaming fans. When teams from smaller towns are playing on a rival's home turf, the entire town shuts down to travel with the team.

The game itself provides the purpose for the gathering, but the supporting casts of cheerleaders, flag corps, and bands make for a true extravaganza. The football coach is often the highest paid member of the faculty and typically has a staff of assistants and trainers to help him. Once, when a new professional player from Texas was asked how he was able to become a starter so quickly, he explained, "It was easy, the playbook up here is a lot simpler than what I used in high school."

Sadly, at many schools, education can take a back seat to football. In the mid-1980s, Texas school officials attempted to implement minimal academic standards for student athletes. This proposal was met with outrage throughout the state and was quickly rescinded, to be replaced by a "no pass, no play" rule that requires a three game suspension of any student failing a course. Of course, only a teacher with great courage and job security would ever consider failing a star player.

✪

Texas as projected by Hollywood tends to attract people of similar nature. Most who come here fall in love with it and become "naturalized" citizens. A female executive from the northeast who has never been on a horse in her life will soon own a pair of cowboy boots and hat for weekend social occasions. An "import" who has only been in the state a year or two will affect a certain swagger in his walk and talk. A popular bumper sticker sums up the attitude: "I was not born in Texas, but I got here as soon as I could."

It has been said that you cannot enter into any lengthy conversation with an ex-marine or Texan without soon being advised of that fact. Texans take a fierce pride in their state and its image. Any disparaging remark regarding the state will be met with at least a hostile glare—if not with some more active form of defense. Texans love to brag about their state and with some good reason. As Joe Namath once said, "If you can do it, it is not brag, but fact." Despite the ready defense of their home turf, Texans (named after the hospitable Tejas Indians) will go to great lengths to project their friendliness. They are, by and large, demonstrably nice folks.

Certain widely held perceptions about Texans are simply not true. I would guess that for every 10,000 people you see wearing cowboy outfits, only one will be a genuine cowboy. Not every Texan owns a pickup truck, although the state does lead the nation in truck registrations (California is a distant second). Not every Texan carries a gun; and although the percentage of people who do so is higher in Texas than in other parts of the country, they still represent a minority.

While Texas certainly contains its share of both good ol' boys and rednecks (God bless them), most Texans fit neither definition. Many will, however, make every effort to make you believe that they do. While the oil industry is still very important to the state, not all Texans are millionaires or owners of oil wells. And while Midland has the highest number of per capita millionaires in the country, the vast majority of the people in Texas reflect the general population of the nation in economic success.

It may be because of this diversity that you will find ready acceptance into almost all segments of Texas society. People are generally given a hearty welcome whatever their race, creed, or national origin and are accepted until they prove themselves deserving of less. Where else but Texas will you find a country music band called, "Kinky Friedman and His Texas Jew Boys" performing to enthusiastic dance hall audiences made up primarily of rednecks?

When riding in Texas, enjoy Texans in their splendor. Be careful though, if you stay too long, you may begin to walk with a swagger.

A Proud History

The colorful history of Texas makes it what it is today. This chapter will give you a short summary of the story. The size of the state and the different backgrounds of the various regions give each area a particular history of its own. Each individual riding chapter includes a short explanation of the local character, to show what makes that region unique.

Proud of their heritage, most small Texan towns have monuments in the square.

Of course, long before Europeans arrived, roaming tribes of Indians inhabited the region. They left little impact on history because they were either killed or run out of the region by new settlers.

After the Spanish conquistadores discovered the vast riches of Mexico and Peru, they turned their interest north, actively seeking more treasure in the "new world." They found little gold or silver but they did discover a black, slimy substance that smelled bad, but would burn. Although they did not realize it, this crude oil would become the "gold" of Texas. In the middle of the 18th century, Spain tried to settle and cultivate these lands while converting the Indians to Christianity. They established a series of missions and forts *(presidios)* in Texas. The Indians resented the intrusion and threat to their way of life. A series of successful attacks stopped further expansion and caused the Spanish to retrench. The most famous of these old missions, San Antonio de Valero, was established in present-day San Antonio and became a real factor in the future of Texas. Today, this mission is better known as the Alamo.

The Mexican people won their independence from Spain in a bloody revolution in 1821, and the area known as Texas became the northernmost state of the new country. Lacking resources other than raw land, the Mexican government made large land grants, called *empresarios,* to U.S. and European citizens in order to encourage settlement of the area. Promises of almost free land and unlimited potential for development brought scores of U.S. citizens south into Texas. Many of the first settlers moved to Texas to escape hanging or lesser criminal penalties. Others left wives and children behind and "escaped" the bonds of civilization. Most, however, were honest, hard working people looking to better their lot in life. They formed the bedrock of the new society.

While obtaining land in Mexican Texas was cheap, it did have drawbacks. To obtain land, you had to become Catholic, renounce your U.S. citizenship, and pledge your loyalty to Mexico. All official documents had to be in Spanish. The new citizens, called Texicans, soon began talking of revolt and forming their own country. In 1833, the Mexican government decreed that no more U.S. citizens would be accepted into Texas.

In 1835 the Texicans declared their independence from Mexico and General Antonio Lopez de Santa Anna amassed an army and marched north to put down the upstart rebellion. The first battle took place at a mission near San Antonio called the Alamo. An army of more than 5,000 Mexicans surrounded 189 Texicans who fought bravely and held off attempts to overrun the Alamo. After twelve days and 2,000 Mexican casualties, the mission fell and all its defenders were killed. Their defeat proved to be a

The Texas state flag is most often flown on a separate flagpole and at a height equal to the U.S. flag, indicating the widespread belief that the nation of Texas equal in importance to the United States.

rallying point for the rest of the Texicans and the battle cry became, "Remember the Alamo!"

The Mexican army, which had experienced heavy losses, had to maintain long and difficult supply lines. When the two opposing armies met in San Jacinto (near Houston) on April 21, 1836 the Texicans had their victory and freedom. Santa Anna was captured and held for several days. It is rumored that Santa Anna had been slow to enter the battle because he'd been enjoying the intimate company of a mulatto woman. The unofficial anthem of the Lone Star State, *The Yellow Rose of Texas,* was written in her honor.

The republic of Texas lasted only a short ten years before joining the United States. The new republic faced the same difficulties as the Mexicans: lots of land, few people, and almost no money. Cheap land grants encouraged immigration, especially from areas of Europe that had problems of their own. Even today, regions of Texas developed by settlers from Germany and elsewhere have retained unique flavors and heritages.

Meanwhile, Texas continued to battle Indian uprisings as well as constant border disputes with Mexico. The republic needed help, and in 1846 Texas was granted statehood, earning the official assistance of the U.S. government and its troops.

As word of the seemingly unlimited land and opportunities in the new state spread, settlers poured in from both the eastern U.S. and Europe. Today Texas has the largest Czech population in the world outside of Czechoslovakia. Eastern Texas became a major cotton-producing state as plantation owners from the American South moved from depleted lands of

Texas Rangers

As law enforcement officers, Texas Rangers are known the world over, a reputation they have earned throughout their storied history, which is rooted in their early attempts to enforce the law along the border. The Mexicans of the 1800s called the rangers *los diablos tejanos,* the Texan devils! The rangers were known to shoot first and ask questions later. Let's just say that protecting the civil rights of a Mexican caught with a few "stray" cattle did not rate high on their list of priorities.

Using similar tactics, the rangers are credited with running the wild Indian tribes from the state, as well as protecting settlers from outlaws. Once, when a town had been overrun by bad guys, the governor was asked to send help to stop the riot. When a single ranger arrived, the city fathers asked, "Only one ranger?" To which the ranger replied, "There is only one riot isn't there?"

It is probably safe to say that most of the early rangers would not be welcome in your living room today. During the Mexican-American war, General Taylor was incensed by the behavior of the rangers. They would kill at any chance and had no regard for the lives of their victims. However, Taylor wanted them at the front in all attacks because they proved themselves up to any task. The early rangers served six-month enlistments and were often not supplied by the government with necessary food and supplies. They solved this problem by "obtaining" any requirements on the spot and promising that the government would reimburse the owner later.

Today, the Texas Rangers are a small, elite force limited to no more than 99 in number. While their primary purpose is guarding the state governor, they also handle white-collar crime investigations and are called out for other special tasks as needed or requested. Texans will speak with great pride of the job Captain Barry Caver did in handling a standoff with Richard McLaren and his followers in 1997. All hostages were released and the group finally surrendered without any loss of life. Compare that to a similar situation handled by the federal government: the debacle in Waco, Texas. ✪

their eastern plantations to the "new" soil of Texas. During the Civil War, Texas sided with the Confederacy and was a major supplier of food and cotton for export. Spurred by the conflict, large-scale cattle production—and the legend of the Texan cowboy—was born.

A stop at the location of the famous Spindletop oil discovery is a "must."

When most people think of Texas history, they picture cowboys, cattle, lawlessness, and gunfights. Its popularity with Hollywood notwithstanding, the wild era of ranchers and outlaws really lasted only about 40 years or so (1860–1900) and was soon squelched by civilizing forces. Continued immigration from more settled states and countries brought about an agricultural boom and the Texas "wheeler-dealer" soon made his appearance to claim a piece of the growing pie. But the expansion of the railroads into cow country ended the need for long drives and barbed wire made it possible to fence off great areas of land at minimal cost.

Civilization may have tamed Texas, but its wild roots run deep. Texans have proudly absorbed this legacy into their daily outlook and you will see it expressed in many ways, from their willingness to take risks, both in life and business, to their generally "loose" attitude toward following The Rules.

We cannot speak of Texas without mentioning oil and its influence. Oil wells were drilled in east Texas as early as 1866. As several small fields were discovered, the business expanded slowly into other parts of the state. Not many uses for oil and oil products existed at the time. In 1901 a well that was drilled near Beaumont, in an area known as Spindletop, would affect the oil industry for nearly 70 years. This well, a "gusher," came in as no other had ever before. When it was finally under control, it could produce more than 80,000 barrels of oil per day—an unprecedented amount. Soon drillers, wildcatters, wheeler-dealers, and lots of other people looking to make money headed to Texas. The era of the oil-field boomtowns must have been quite a sight to see. Tales of whores, gambling dens, saloons, shootings, knifings, and other unsavory activities abound.

By the 1960s, while oil was still king, the Texas economy was starting to diversify as people flocked to Texas, attracted by the warm climate, inexpensive housing, friendly reputation, and dreams of a better life. As it is known in Texas, this "Yankee Invasion" did little to change attitudes in the state. Most new arrivals promptly got a pair of cowboy boots, a cowboy hat, and a pickup truck and were soon absorbed into the culture. While still leader of the House, Lyndon Johnson was a master in the art of "pork barrel" politics. He managed to get several military bases located in Texas and was instrumental in NASA's decision to locate its headquarters near Houston. This obviously attracted many other high-tech companies with huge government contracts to move to the state. True to their nature, Texans soon became experts in land and real estate speculation.

Since the oil embargo of 1973, imposed by the Organization of Petroleum Exporting Countries (OPEC), Texas and its oil industry have gone through several "boom and bust" economic periods. Texans have reacted to these cycles true to the form of their forefathers. They picked themselves up, dusted off their pants, and went in search of the next opportunity. By the early 1990s Texans had diversified their economy away from the oil industry, although it still plays an important role. Their high-tech industry rivals California's famous Silicon Valley. With the passing of NAFTA, business with Mexico increased and Texas led all states in population growth during the '90s.

One can only wonder what Texas will do next.

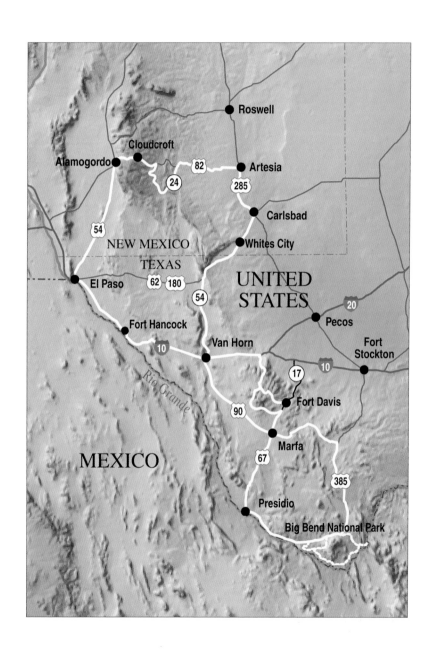

Wild West Texas

Beginning and ending in El Paso, this eight-day route of approximately 1,100 miles will take you through some of the most remote areas in the lower 48 states. The vastness of west Texas can be overwhelming and occasional stops alongside the road gives a person time to reflect on one's small place in the world. The area offers some great mountain riding, dual sport options, and opportunities to see several natural wonders. Visits to towns of less than 1,000 inhabitants will give you some insight into the sort of people who have chosen this lonely, wide open space as their home.

The area's desert environment and sheer remoteness made it one of the last parts of Texas to become civilized. Outlaws, bandits, gunslingers, and other ne'er-do-wells controlled the area until 1916 when the U.S. Army under the command of **General "Black Jack" Pershing** took control at Fort Bliss and finally brought order to the entire area.

El Paso sits in a valley with the Franklin mountains invitingly close by.
(photo by J. Griffis/TxDOT)

Today's cowboy boots, while still maintaining their original, functional design, are most often only a fashion statement. (photo by J. Griffis Smith/ TxDOT)

Today, west Texas still contains immense open spaces with some of the sparsest population densities in the United States, as well as the world's largest bi-national metropolis, **El Paso-Juárez**, with the population of the greater metropolitan area approaching four million people. The two cities in the metropolis exist almost as one, with constant traffic between the two during all hours of the day, year-round. U.S. citizens cross the border to obtain less expensive health care and goods, as well as to enjoy the freer lifestyles of Mexico; Mexican citizens come to El Paso to obtain goods and services not available on the Mexican side.

With the implementation of the North American Free Trade Agreement, many factories, called *maquiladoras,* have been built with U.S. capital and management to take advantage of cheaper labor rates of Mexico. Unlike other cities in Texas, El Paso does not have a major tourist draw, but people come to El Paso to enjoy easy access to Mexico and the remote desert. The **Franklin Mountains,** at the end of the Rockies chain, form the northern boundary of the city and they offer wonderful opportunities for the residents to enjoy the rugged outdoors.

El Paso is the cowboy boot capitol of the world. If you hanker for a set of boots at a good price, try **Cowtown Boots** at 11451 Gateway West (915-593-2929). With more than 40,000 square feet of western wear, they have something for everyone. Craftsmen in the "bootmaking" district of El Paso, located along S. Cotton Street, offer custom-made creations that can top $10,000 a pair.

Cowboy Boots

The cowboy boot originated in Spain, migrated to Mexico, and found its home in Texas. They were originally designed to be a functional piece of rugged footwear: the pointed toe makes it easy to put your foot in a stirrup, the heel gives you some stability while riding, and the high tops are meant to protect the wearer from thorns and other hazards of the range. Today, of course, the cowboy boot has become a fashion statement. Until the 1960s, almost all cowboy boots were handmade. Today, Texas is the world's leader in cowboy boot production. One company alone has annual sales of more than three million pairs. In Paris, Texas, there is even a tombstone with a statue of Jesus wearing cowboy boots.

The cost of a pair of boots is first determined by whether they are factory or hand made. Custom fitting and your choice of materials and designs will all contribute to the cost. A good, "off the shelf" pair will probably be $200–300; a serviceable hand-made pair will be a little more expensive, but not much. Of course, top-of-the-line cowboy boots made with detailed inlays and exotic skins, such as ostrich, eel, or anaconda, can run $5,000 or more. Two of the more popular designs include the Texas Lone Star and derricks gushing crude oil. Because of the high demand, custom boot orders from the best craftsmen can take more than a year to fill.   ✪

EL PASO EXCURSIONS

If possible, you should take a ride on the **Trans Mountain Loop** (Loop 375) that goes across the Franklin Mountains and through **Franklin Mountains State Park**. Take I-10 west to Exit 6 (Canutilo) and follow it to its conclusion at the intersection with Hwy. 54. Take a right here and you will re-enter El Paso on the eastern side. The total ride is about 32 miles, downtown to downtown, and the 12-mile loop road itself is a delight. The climb to almost 7,000 feet has pull-offs overlooking the twin cities.

Two interesting sites are situated almost side by side on the eastern end of the Trans Mountain Loop. The first is the **Border Patrol Museum** (4315 Trans Mountain Road), which outlines the history of this organization and houses exhibits of items confiscated from people trying to enter the United States illegally. Second is the **El Paso Museum of Archaeology** at 4332 Trans Mountain Road (915-755-4332), closed Mondays. It exhibits the

When pulling over to the side of the road for a break, always keep a sharp eye out for these "natives," as they are found throughout all of Texas in great numbers. (photo by Jack Lewis/TxDOT)

flora of the desert that you will soon visit along a self-guided outdoor trail. It also has an indoor section that details the lives of the early Indian inhabitants. The two museums are connected by a footpath.

Another way to visit the Franklin Mountains is to take the **Wyler Aerial Tramway** (915-556-6622), with guides along to point out the various sights while you enjoy the spectacular views. From the visitors' center, you can see New Mexico and the Mexican state of Chihuahua. To get to the tram, take U.S. 54 north to the Fred Wilson Boulevard which turns into Alabama Sreet, follow Alabama and take a right on McKinley which ends at the park.

Another short ride that can provide you with a real sense of history is the **Mission Trail.** Call the trail association at 915-534-0677 to get information about events and guided tours. Take I-10 east from downtown to the Zaragoza exit (32). Turn right on Zaragoza to Old Pueblo Road, which will place you on the clearly marked trail in Ysleta. **Ysleta del Sur Pueblo** offers quite a contrast to the visitor, with the oldest mission in Texas sitting right next to a huge casino complex. The **Tigua Cultural Center,** home of the Tigua Indian tribe, at 305 Yaya Lane, gives wonderful insight into the lives

Just How Dry is West Texas?
The amount of rainfall received in Texas varies greatly. In the east, more than fifty inches a year is common. This diminishes steadily as you move west, and west Texas receives only a few inches per year. Starting at about the Dallas-Fort Worth area, there would not be enough rainfall to support agriculture or cattle if it were not for huge, underground lakes, called aquifers, whose water levels are carefully monitored and guarded. Historically, water rights are precious and they have been the subject of lawsuits or shootings. When you are out and about, be sure to stay adequately hydrated.   ✪

of these people and how they have managed to retain their culture over the years. Two miles further east on the trail (Hwy. 20), you will come to the **Socorro Mission,** the oldest continually active parish in the United States (est. 1681). Another five miles east, the small town of San Elizario contains the **San Elizario Presido** (1521 San Elizario Rd.). A visit to the church established here in 1877 and a stroll about the town square will remind you of many similar small towns in Mexico. A small visitor's center and museum give insight to the historical significance of these missions. Turn north, left, to return to the Interstate and El Paso.

EL PASO LODGING

El Paso offers lodgings in every price range with most of the national chains represented in the airport area. There are also many "mom and pop" motels near the airport that provide cheap, basic lodging. *Sandy's Choice:* If you would like something special try the **Casa de Sueños** (house of dreams), 405 Mountain Vista Rd., (www.casaofdreams.com, 575-874-9166, double rooms start at $100). This bed and breakfast is located just a few minutes outside the west side of town off exit 8 on I-10. With only four rooms and setting in a quiet desert area, you can begin to experience your upcoming desert adventure while still exploring the city.

Primitive camping is available at **Franklin Mountains State Park,** 1331 McKelligon Canyon Rd., (915-566-6441), two sites only. The only other camping available is approximately 20 miles outside the city on Hwy. 180/62, left on FM 2775 at **Hueco State Historical Site,** (915-849-6684). Park tables, grills, water, and toilet facilities are available here. Reservations are required to be made two days in advance.

EL PASO DINING

Your dining options are almost limitless in and around El Paso. Not only is it the self-proclaimed Mexican Food Capitol of the U.S., it is also renowned for its steak houses. One of my favorite places for carving up a cow can be found on the western outskirts of town. The **State Line** (915-581-3377) so named because the border between New Mexico and Texas runs through the middle of the place, is located off I-10 west of downtown at 1222 Sunland Park Drive. If you have a hearty appetite, consider one of their all-you-can-eat platters—just make sure you will be able to remount your bike when you're done.

Be sure to take some time out from your ride through west Texas to enjoy the scenery.

Cowboys

While the cowboy played a brief but important role in Texas, Hollywood has inflated their true significance completely out of proportion with history. Even at their peak, cowboys represented only a minuscule portion of the population.

After the Civil War, Texas had both vast, free-roaming herds of cattle and a growing market for them in the east. The rough and rugged men who rounded up these herds to drive them to the nearest railroad claimed their stock by branding them. A cowboy's life was difficult, and the work hard and dirty. At the end of a drive, they would draw their pay and let their hair down in wild towns where just about anything could happen, and often did, giving rise to yet another historical icon, that of the Texas lawman.

With the advent of barbed wire and the extension of the railroads, long cattle drives became obsolete and the cowboy all but disappeared from the landscape—but not the silver screen. Today, you will see lots of Texans wearing cowboy boots and hats, but few cowboys. ✪

Day 1 El Paso to Fort Hancock

Distance *50 miles*

Features *This day is designed to let you arrive in El Paso, pick up your bike, and get out of the city. Or you can spend the day sightseeing and still get out of the city and on your way. The Mission Trail (described above) is along the route as you leave town. Although Interstate riding is not the most exciting, it is the most efficient way to get to the meat of this route. Besides, it gives you a good introduction to the wide-open spaces and desert highlands of this region.*

From looking at this sign, it would appear these riders have been having a good time. (courtesy of MotoDiscovery)

From El Paso, get on I-10 east and go to the town of Fort Hancock (Exit 72). The **Fort Hancock Motel** ($60; 915-769-3981), just off the interstate on the right, is a good clean "mom and pop" place. Ask for a room in the rear. Standing outside your room in the evening, the seemingly endless views across the desert to the mountains in the distance and the yelping of coyotes will let you know that you have arrived in west Texas!

Across the street from the Fort Hancock is the non-descript **Angie's Café.** While this place is a hole-in-the-wall, the food is wonderful and it has been written up in *National Geographic Explorer, Texas Monthly,* and other well-regarded travel publications. If you plan to eat only one Texas chicken-fried steak on your trip, this is the place!

Day 2 Fort Hancock to Fort Davis

Distance *160 miles*

Features *This day starts with another 100 miles or so of interstate riding across the seemingly endless desert highlands before turning south into the Davis Mountains. From there, you will enjoy wonderful up-and-down twisties. As you approach 7,000 feet you will leave the desert behind for rugged forests. Note that you will enter the Central Time Zone shortly before passing Van Horn at Exit 140.*

The tour through the McDonald Observatory will have your mind reeling at the vastness of the universe.

Continue on I-10 to Exit 176 at Kent. Turn south on Hwy. 118. After 20 miles or so, you enter the Davis Mountains and pass the **University of Texas McDonald Observatory** (www.mcdonaldobservatory.org) on your left, at an altitude of nearly 7,000 feet, before descending into the town of Fort Davis (population 1,050) for the night. At just over 5,000 feet, Fort Davis is the highest city in Texas. I recommend you stop at the observatory on your way by to see which tours and activities might best fit your schedule tomorrow.

The town of **Fort Davis** was founded in 1854 on the **Overland Trail** between San Antonio and El Paso. It must have been a pleasant stop for the many settlers, gold seekers, and others heading west to find better times, as they left the crushing heat of the desert and ascended to these cooler altitudes. Even today, its economy supports the many tourists seeking an opportunity to get out of their air-conditioned environments and enjoy the outdoors during the summer months. A short stroll off the main street will allow you to see how the residents lived in the old days, with traditional adobe houses still in use today.

As you enter Fort Davis, you will soon see *(Sandy's Choice)* the **Hotel**

This rider appears to be contemplating a U-turn to ride the Davis Mountain loop again—tempting!

Limpia (www.hotellimpia.com, 432-426-3237, 800-662-5517, $100) on your left at the town square. This delightfully restored hotel was originally built in 1884 near the site of the fort itself, but was moved to its "new" location in 1912, where it provided lodging for rich folks from the hot flatlands seeking cool air in the summertime. Although it has been finished throughout in period décor from the early 1900s, the rooms have all the modern conveniences. In 1953 a fire destroyed the lobby and the hotel was reconfigured into apartments and office space rented to Harvard University for faculty and students using the observatory. Then in 1978 it was reconverted into a hotel with the original style. The adjoining restaurant offers great dining at a level you might not expect to find in such a small town.

As an alternative, the **Old Texas Inn** ($60; 432-426-3118) has six rooms with all amenities but also decorated in period décor. It is located on the main drag as you enter town above the **Fort Davis Drug Store**, which now serves as a souvenir stand and a local café that serves up some good ol' west Texas cooking. There are several other more standard motels in this town, but a stay in either of these will give you a taste of what it was like in this area at the turn of the century.

If you are camping, return to Hwy. 118 going north. The entrance to **Davis Mountains State Park** (915-426-3337), is only three miles back at Park Road 3. With a wonderful atmosphere on the Limpia River, the park offers more than 90 sites, all with water, a barbeque grill, and tables. Hot showers and restrooms are available. The **Indian Lodge Motel** is within the park and has adequate dining facilities.

You"ll see boulders the size of small houses throughout the Davis Mountains.

Day 3 Fort Davis to Presidio

Distance *155 miles*

Features *This 72-mile loop through the Davis Mountains will give you ample chance to twist your wrist and scrape your pegs, though a more leisurely pace will allow for roadside stops to soak in the beautiful mountain scenery. I recommend you get off your bike to visit Fort Davis (a National Historical Landmark) and the University of Texas McDonald Observatory (see details below). A 60-mile run through remote high desert will put you in the small town of Presidio at the Mexican border.*

This biker can only hope he doesn't encounter the cowboy who fits these spurs. (photo by Jack Binion)

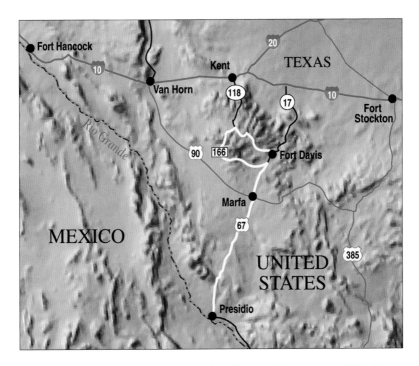

Leave town the way you came in, and at the outskirts, on your left, the restored **Fort Davis** awaits your visit. As more people began using the **Overland Trail** from San Antonio to El Paso, raids from the Apache and Comanche Indians became a problem. In 1854 the U.S. Army established a fort near the Limpia River to escort wagon trains through the area, pursue Indian raiders, and guard the mail. Named in honor of **Jefferson Davis,** the Secretary of War at the time, the facility was built of cottonwood, scrub oak, and pine; today only the foundations of the original fort remain. It was abandoned, occupied by Confederates during the Civil War, and abandoned again before being reconstructed in adobe and stone in 1867. The famous **"buffalo soldiers,"** all-black units with white officers, occupied the fort during the 1870s and '80s. It was closed in 1891.

In 1961 Fort Davis was designated as a **National Historic Site** and has been faithfully restored as one of the best surviving examples of a southwestern frontier military post. A nice museum is located inside, and a short film tracing the history of the fort is shown throughout the day. You are welcome to roam at will. The interiors of several of the buildings have been restored and reflect the living conditions of the day.

After your visit, continue to retrace yesterday's route for about 15 miles. The **University of Texas McDonald Observatory** complex will be on your

By stopping by and visiting the Fort Davis National Historical Site, you gain real insights into life on the frontier. (photo by Jack Lewis/TxDOT)

right. It is hard to miss, as you can spot the enormous buildings containing the telescopes for miles before arriving. At an altitude of approximately 6,800 feet, the observatory is located in one of the "darkest" parts of the United States (i.e. little interference from man-made artificial light sources). The original 84-inch telescope was constructed in 1938 by the University of Texas and was then the second largest in existence. A 107-inch scope was completed in 1969 as a joint project of the University of Texas and NASA. The 13.5-million dollar **Hobby Eberly Telescope,** dedicated in October of 1997, contains 91 hexagonal mirrors over a 36-foot wide surface and is the world's largest mirror telescope. Harvard University also has a world-renowned radio telescope located at the site. Time on the telescopes is booked months and years in advance by researchers from all over the world.

Since the facility cannot be used during daylight hours for scientific study, the time is set aside to give guided tours to the general public. A short video is shown throughout the day outlining the physical facilities and the work that is done here. You can also look at the sun to view sunspots and flares.

Many interesting events, including "star parties" are offered on some

The University of Texas' McDonald Observatory telescopes can be seen from miles away.

evenings (go to www.mcdonaldobservatory.org or call 915-426-3640 for a schedule). Most presentations are on a first-come, first-served basis and rarely are full, but evening "star parties" often require reservations well in advance. Note that if you want to attend one of the latter, be extremely careful riding to and from the site after dark, as wildlife is copious and the road leading up to the site, known as **Skyline Drive**, is the highest paved road in Texas. With all the clear air, it seems you can see forever.

From this point, another 15 miles north on Hwy. 118 will bring you to the intersection of Hwy. 166, a scenic loop which will return you to the

The Davis Mountains await you with some truly enjoyable riding.

town of Fort Davis after 45 miles or so. Just outside Fort Davis you will come to a T-intersection with Hwy. 17; turn right toward Marfa, only 20 miles down the road. At this point, the **Davis Mountains** will be in your rear view mirror as you cross pastureland and farms. The huge greenhouses along this drive are hydroponic tomato farms which specialize in a hybrid variety named after Fort Davis. One operation, Ft. Davis Division, consists of more than 40 acres of fields with a 76,000-square-foot packing plant that ships more than 20 million pounds of tomatoes annually.

Follow Hwy. 17 signs through **Marfa** until you intersect with Hwy. 67. Take Hwy. 67 south toward **Presidio**. This is a quick 59-mile ride through the desert with mountains jutting up on every side and Mexico straight ahead. Approximately 35 miles south of Marfa, a dirt road off to the right leads to the much-acclaimed **Cibolo Creek Ranch** (www.cibolo-creekranch.com, 866-496-9460), a truly wonderful 25,000-acre dude ranch *(Sandy's Choice)*. At more than $300 per night (includes meals), it should be good. Developed by Milton Faver in the mid-19th century, the ranch contains a series of forts surrounding the main ranch house for protection from the Indians and bandits. It is now a popular retreat for celebrities and the rich.

Past the ranch turnoff the road becomes more interesting with nice curves and gently rolling hills. In Presidio, the **Three Palms Hotel** (915-229-3611, $60), located on old Hwy. 67 north, is more than adequate. Next door to the motel is the **Oasis Café**, which is very popular with locals and serves up some good Tex-Mex food. Primitive camping is available only a short distance to the east on Hwy. 170 in the **Big Bend Ranch State Park** near the **Fort Leaton State Historic Site**. The campsite has pit toilets only, but water and showers are available.

Presidio (pop. 4,000) is known as the hottest town in Texas. Its twin on the Mexico side is Ojinaga and the two towns co-exist as if one. This is the only official border crossing point between El Paso and Del Rio, a 450-mile stretch. The area contains fertile floodplains and is famous for its farming. It is the self-proclaimed **Onion Capitol of the World**. It is important as the western entryway to **El Camino del Rio** (River Road), which has been touted as one of the ten best motorcycle roads in the United States.

Side Trip to Ojinaga

Should you wish to visit Mexico, the town of **Ojinaga** (pop. 40,000) just across the river from Presidio is a good place to do so easily and safely. No paperwork is required if you plan to stay less than 72 hours and do not continue on into the interior. As of this writing, the document requirements to enter Mexico on land were in a state of flux. It is suggested that you check on the current situation before leaving home. It is not recommended that you take your bike across as parking and leaving it while you shop or explore tends to attract the unsavory element that seem to accumulate in all border cities. The easiest way to visit Ojinaga is to simply walk across the border, or take a cab which will cost about seven dollars.

Ojinaga is not a tourist town, but has a thriving international trade. Try eating "real" Mexican food at **La Problana** (Calle Juaraz near the Zocolo). Not to be missed is **Panderia La Francesa** on Calle Zaragoza near the town plaza, where you can stock up on sweets for your late night snack or morning meal.

Day 4 Presidio to Big Bend National Park

Distance *120 miles*

Features *Don't let the distance fool you. You will be stopping often and spending much time on the side of the road enjoying the magnificent landscape. The 50-mile stretch from Presidio to Lajitas curves constantly as it follows the path of the Rio Grande River. You will climb the steepest hill in Texas—a 16-percent grade to a height of 5,000 feet. After reaching Study Butte you will enter the Big Bend National Park with its astonishing terrain and roads. The day ends in the Chisos Basin.*

Depart the motel, return to Hwy. 170 and continue for 67 miles on Hwy. 170 eastward to Study Butte. This road from Presidio to Study Butte is often mentioned by various publications as one of the ten most scenic roads in the United States, and most motorcyclists would agree with the designation. After 46 miles of delightful riding, you will encounter "the hill." At a 16-percent grade, this hill is the steepest in Texas and the road peaks at an altitude of more than 5,000 feet. There is a nice pull-off at the summit and

This rider sure has come to the right place to test his dual-sport skills.

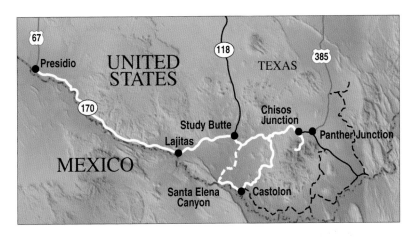

only the hard-core, no-photos-please rider will be able to resist the urge to burn a good deal of film there. Walk over the summit and get the view ahead before remounting your bike for the five-mile run to Lajitas.

The small outpost of **Lajitas** was established because it had an easy crossing over the **Rio Grande River**, and over the years it served this purpose well for Indians, traders, and *banditos* alike. In the early 1900s **General "Black Jack" Pershing** established a U.S. Cavalry post here to deal with **Pancho Villa** and his band.

For years Lajitas was a sleepy little desert town populated by a few seeking solitude. Then in 2000 the entire city including 25,000 surrounding acres was purchased by an Austin multimillionaire who had visions of making it into the ultimate exclusive retreat for the rich and famous. After $100 million were spent in development costs, the whole deal went into bankruptcy and was purchased by another wealthy Texan for only 13.5 million in late 2007. The plan is to take the luxury upgrades originally designed for the upper class and let us "regulars" in. The jury is still out. You do have to admire these Texans and their dreams though. The resort consists of a period style square containing several stores, hotels, and restaurants. Accommodations range in cost from $200 to $1,000 per night and include apartments and condos. An eighteen-hole golf course is available.

Only one remnant of the "real" Lajitas exists and continues to do well, Henry Clay III, third generation mayor and goat with living accommodations in the old **Lajitas Trading Post.** Several years back, in a hotly contested mayoral race, the citizens of Lajitas chose a goat named **Henry Clay** as the winner. Henry's main claim to fame, other than being mayor, was his ability to consume vast quantities of beer. Henry died, some say of liver failure, and was succeeded by his son, **Henry, Jr.** Unfortunately, Henry Jr. eventually

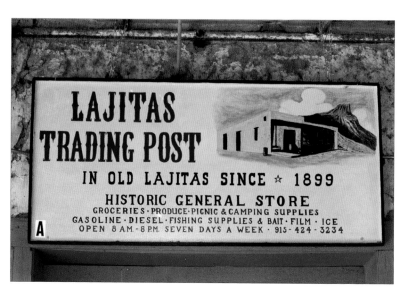

This is not a tourist trap, but a genuine general store in Lajitas.
(courtesy of MotoDiscovery)

met the same fate. The grandson, **Henry Clay III** carries on the family tradition today, although a former political opponent, frustrated after losing election after election to a goat, decided to vent his spleen by castrating Henry III in hopes that it would put an end to this political dynasty.

From Lajitas it is only 17 miles to the intersection with Farm Road 118 at **Study Butte** (all services). Turn right and it's only a short ride to the **Big Bend National Park** entrance ($15 fee).

After passing the entrance booth into the park, take an immediate right turn onto Old Maverick Road. This is 13 miles of well-maintained dirt that is easily traveled by any bike with competent rider. Take a minute to dismount six or seven miles down this road. The silence will overwhelm most people. Think of the hardships that must have been incurred trying to cross this empty desert land on a horse or wagon.

When you intersect with pavement again, turn right for a mile or so to the dead-end at **Santa Elena Canyon.** A short hike allows you to climb up and into the canyon, which was cut by the **Rio Grande River.** Its sheer cliffs, which reach more than 1,500 feet above the Rio Grande, and narrow passages will amaze you. Plan to spend some time here to explore and enjoy. Should you not wish to ride this short dirt portion, at Maverick Junction continue on pavement for 13 miles to Santa Elena Junction and make a right turn. It is then 30 paved miles to the Santa Elena Canyon.

After enjoying the wonderful sights and sounds of Santa Elena, take the paved road out and return 30 miles to the main road. This road out of Santa Elena to the main road is an absolute pleasure, with sprinklings of buttes and broad valleys. There are several well-marked pull-offs along this road provided by the park service with informative signs. One of the best is the **Mule Ears viewpoint.**

At the main road turn right and continue about 10 miles to Chisos Mountains Basin Junction where a right turn will take you to the **Chisos Basin.** If the entranceway booth was closed as you entered the park, you will need to proceed straight ahead for another three miles to the **Panther**

The Rio Grande River created the Santa Elena Canyon which now cuts a dramatic swath on the southern border of the Big Bend National Park. (photo by Jack Lewis/ TxDOT)

*Roads in the Big Bend Park offer frequent pull-offs containing interesting exhibits.
(photo by Jack Binion).*

Junction Visitors' Center to get your admission tickets, before continuing back to the **Chisos Lodge** for your overnight accommodations. At the park headquarters at Panther Junction you can obtain brochures, maps, and other information that will make your visit more enjoyable.

If you already have paid the entrance fee, the same information is available at the **Chisos Basin Visitor Center.** The short, six-mile ride into the basin is a beautiful motorcycle road that climbs up over the mountain. It is quite tight at some places and even has a couple of switchbacks. Other than campsites, the **Chisos Mountains Lodge** (www.chisosmountainlodge.com, 915-477-2291/866-875-8456, $115) is the only available place to overnight in the park and offers a dramatic setting. It has 66 motel-type rooms and *(Sandy's Choice)* six stone cottages ($150) located only a short walk away. Deer, wild pigs, and other wildlife can be seen in the early evenings and mornings as you walk to the basic, but adequate, dining room. At times, most notably during Spring Break, the place can be filled; it is best to call ahead and reserve a room.

Camping is available in Big Bend on a first-come basis at Rio Grande Village, Chisos Basin, and Castolon, at a cost of $14 per night. All "formal" campsites have showers and water. Chisos Basin offers high-country camping with the lodge located just up the hill with café service. It also has a well-stocked store to meet most of your needs. Rio Grande, as the name implies, is located on the banks of the Rio Grande River, nestled among trees. Backcountry campsites are free, but do require a permit. Before spending the night at a remote campsite, make sure you get current information at the ranger station.

Big Bend National Park is often called **The Last Frontier of Texas** (info 915-477-2251; res. 915-477-2291). Containing more than 800,000 acres, the park is larger than the state of Rhode Island, yet it's also one of the least visited parks in the country. Be prepared both for long, remote stretches without amenities, as well as some of the best motorcycling you will have ever encountered. Much of the Big Bend is **Chihuahuan Desert,** but the **Chisos Mountains,** located in the center of the park, rise to more than 7,000 feet in altitude. In the south, the Rio Grande River has cut deep canyons full of cane groves and rich vegetation. Many people spend weeks exploring this area and its natural beauty. The Indians say that when God was finished creating the world, he placed all the leftover rocks in the Big Bend. After your visit, you may be a believer. Note that the rich wildlife of the area is not all friendly toward man: bears, mountain lions, rattlesnakes, huge spiders, and scorpions all call the Big Bend home.

Optional Dual-Sport Day Exploring River Roads

Distance *104 miles (54 paved, 50 dirt)*

Features *If you have a dual-sport bike, you'll want to take an optional day to explore the hinterlands. Big Bend offers some excellent opportunities to get out into the backcountry. Off-road riding is not allowed, but a series of great dirt roads await you. This is a full day's ride, so plan accordingly.*

The remote dirt roads in the Big Bend Park allows one to really get away from it all.

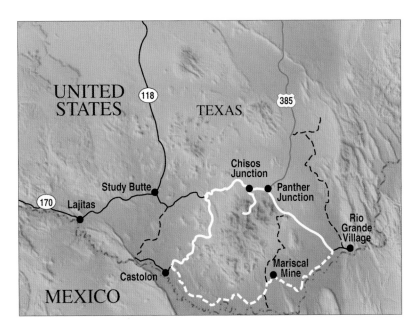

None of the unpaved roads in the Big Bend are technically difficult, but they would be best enjoyed with a dual-sport bike. Check with the local ranger station before heading out to learn about current hazards and weather conditions. Be sure to carry plenty of water, and make sure someone knows your route and when you plan to return. If you should encounter problems, your best bet will be to stay with your bike and wait for someone to come along—usually it will be only an hour or two. Unless you are sure that you are near the end of one of these roads, do not try to walk out. As always with dual-sport riding, a partner is recommended.

These backroads offer so many opportunities for stops and side trips that it is almost impossible to list them all. If you want to explore, I suggest you purchase the *Road Guide to Backcountry Dirt Roads of Big Bend National Park,* available at the park headquarters. Throughout the area, be on the lookout for mountain lions, bobcat, deer, and wild pigs. Most of the wildlife is very shy and you will have to be very observant to spot one of these animals. Rattlesnakes, however, should be given a wide berth.

Leaving the Chisos Basin, return to the main road and turn left. After about 10 miles, turn left toward Santa Elena Canyon and retrace your route of the previous day until just before the village of Castolon (approx. 20 miles) where the left turn onto dirt is clearly marked as the **River Road West**. You will then begin a 50-mile ride that will really put you into the heart of Big Bend.

The Indians believed that when God was through creating the world, he put all the leftover rocks in the Big Bend

After about six miles on dirt, you will reach a highpoint that allows a wonderful view of the **Santa Elena Canyon**, thirteen miles in the distance. Stop, take your picture, and enjoy the loneliness. Another nine miles will bring you to the ruins of the **Johnson Ranch.** This is the largest set of ruins in the park and a visit to the graveyard will lead most to think of the people who lived their entire lives in this remote area. There are several campsites along the road; permits are available at the ranger station.

Twenty-seven miles after entering the dirt, you will encounter some of the most difficult riding. Hang in there. This stretch only lasts for a few short miles. Also at about twenty-seven miles, you will find the turn off to the **Talley Ranch.** This six-mile side trip will take you to the Rio Grande, the ruins of the Talley Ranch and a favorite camping spot for many.

After 30 miles, it is very important that you take the right turn toward the Mariscal Mine. If you miss this turn, you will end up on some unmaintained roads that can really test your abilities. Should you feel up to it, try going straight at the Mariscal Mine turn off onto Black Gap Road. After nine miles of this road, most folks will welcome the right turn to reconnect with the River Road East. When you hit pavement again, turn left and return to the Chisos Basin for a shower and bed.

After thirty-two miles of dirt, you will reach the **Mariscal Mine,** the site of a mercury mine that existed from 1900 until 1923. Today we are warned about handling any of the dirt or other things in the area due to the possibility of mercury poisoning. One can only wonder what the Mexican laborers at this mine endured. Seven miles after the Mariscal Mine turn, take the left turn on River Road East to Hot Springs and Rio Grande Village. Continue through this beautiful, but harsh, desert until you find pavement just north of **Rio Grande Village.**

You should be careful when encountering a javelina (wild pig) as they can turn nasty when annoyed. (photo by Bill Reeves/TxDOT)

Day 6 Big Bend to Marfa

Distance *160 miles (via pavement), 150 miles (via the alternate route)*
Features *Today, you will be exploring the eastern side of Big Bend, either via dirt or pavement. The historic Gage hotel in Marathon is worth a stop. Wide-open spaces, wild-west towns, and wonderful people will make this a day to remember.*

From Chisos Basin, return to the main road and turn right toward Panther Junction. From Panther Junction it is only twenty miles to the village of Rio Grande, which consists of a gas station and snack store. But in addition to the great road in, two things make it worth the trip: the hot springs and the overlook at Baquillas Canyon.

The well-marked right turn to the hot springs will take you down a two-mile side road. The naturally occurring **hot springs** are only a short walk down a well-maintained trail and there are almost always others around enjoying the spot. Bring your bathing suit. After a good soak, you should then continue on the main road through the tunnel to the left turn toward **Baquillas**, at the eastern end of **Big Bend National Park.** It is possible to cross the Rio Grande into Mexico via a small boat, but there really is not much on the Mexican side, unless you want a beer. Backtrack to Panther Junction and take Hwy. 385 north toward Marathon.

The hot springs in the Big Bend Park offer a refreshing stop for all.
(photo by Jack Binion)

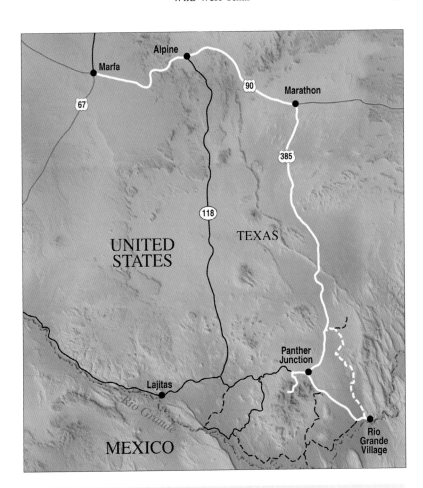

Dual-Sport Option

On your return from Baquillas, turn right just past the tunnel
onto the Old Ore Road for 26 miles, then turn left on the Dagger
Flat Road for two miles, and you will reconnect with pavement
near the **Persimmon Gap** entrance at the north end of the park.
The Old Ore Road was the main road for hauling ore to Marathon.
As this route changes in elevation, notice how the vegetation
changes, too. Several abandoned ranch houses and mining ruins
are along this road, usually located near springs (identified by lush
flora and in one case, old water tanks). These are always good
places to look for wildlife. Note that this dirt road is not for the
faint-hearted; a lot of sand sits in the washes. But it's fun!

Should your schedule permit, an overnight at the Gage Hotel in Marathon is a treat. (photo by Jack Binion)

After exiting the park, continue on Hwy. 385. In forty miles, at the junction with Hwy. 90 at Marathon, turn left toward Marfa. This road, though flat and straight, leads you through the **Santiago** and **Woods Hollow Mountains** and makes for a great ride. Keep your eye out for low-flying Air Force planes practicing maneuvers.

Marathon (pop. 800) is a typical small, west Texas town in that it has most of the services needed for survival, but little else. The crown jewel in Marathon is the **Gage Hotel,** built in 1927 by Alfred Gage, a rancher who once had a 500,000-acre ranch in the area and needed a place to house his frequent guests and visiting business associates. It was renovated in 1978 and is decorated and furnished in period fashion. Rooms range from "basic"—bath down the hall, to "nice"—bath in the room, to "wonderful"— private suites with fireplaces *(Sandy's Choice).* It is fairly pricey with rates from $85 to $300, but it is worth stopping just to look around. While all the rooms are in 1920s west Texas ranch décor, they are all different. Consider this a cultural stop.

Fifty-five miles on Hwy. 90 from Marathon will get you to Marfa. About eight miles before arriving in Marfa, note the pull-off area on the left from which you can view the Marfa Lights, as you may wish to return here at night.

As you ride into the town of **Marfa** (pop. 2,500), you will see that the "lights" are the big attraction here and many of the buildings and souvenir shops sport an alien theme. Recently the town has attempted to become sort of an artists' colony and that is attracting a different type of visitor. Marfa also contains a beautiful courthouse constructed from local stone in 1886. Atop the courthouse dome stands a life-sized statue of Lady Justice, though she is missing her scales. A local man who felt that he had not received justice inside, reportedly shot them off upon departing. The movie *Giant* was filmed in Marfa, and the lobby of the **El Paisano Hotel** *(Sandy's Choice)* on 207 N. Highland Avenue (915-729-3145, $100+) displays some of the memorabilia from the film. There are several "mom and pop" type places along Hwy. 90 in the $ 60/70 range in various states of repair. It is recommended that you check your room and amenities carefully before plunking down your cash; keeping in mind that it is only 21 miles up the road to Fort Davis. There are no campsites available in Marfa or nearby.

The **Marfa Lights** are an enigma. They are most often referred to as "those mysterious Marfa Lights." These bright orbs were first noticed by settlers in the late 1800s. They appear, disappear, separate into multiple lights, change color, and move around throughout the year, but are seen most frequently in the fall. Scientists who have studied them for years still have no explanation for them. Perhaps you can figure it out. The locals love their lights and they are one of west Texas' top tourist attractions. Be very careful riding to and from the viewing area, as there is much wildlife along the road at night here.

No one has ever solved the riddle of the mysterious Marfa Lights.

Day 7 Marfa to Whites City, New Mexico

Distance *175 miles*

Features *This will be a day of mostly wide-open riding on flat, straight roads with wonderful views of mountains in the distance. Even though it gets curvier as you climb over the Guadalupe Mountains, it is still high-speed riding. Plan to stop at Carlsbad Caverns National Park in the afternoon.*

Ride west on Hwy. 90 for approximately 73 miles to Van Horn, then take Hwy. 54 north for 55 miles to the intersection with Hwys. 180/62 (straight ahead).

Guadalupe National Park is one of the newest of our national parks, created in 1972, and it receives fewer than 300,000 visitors each year, many of whom come in the fall to see the leaves turn. **Guadalupe Mountain**, at over 8,700 feet in altitude, is the highest point in Texas. The park headquarters, on the left on Hwy. 180/62, offers several exhibits outlining what lives and grows in the park. Rangers are available to answer your questions. There are no lodgings or eating facilities, but camping is allowed on a first-come-first-served basis. As you exit the park to the north, a nice "mom and pop" café, **The Nickel,** has a limited, yet delicious, menu.

From this point, continue on Hwy. 180/62 to **Whites City,** a town that exists solely because it is close to Carlsbad Caverns National Park. In Whites City, there are three **Best Western** motels (800-CAVERNS, $80) on the highway at the intersection with the turn leading to Carlsbad Caverns. They are grouped around a "turn of the west" type strip mall that contains two restaurants, a souvenir shop, grocery store, small museum, and a self-styled "opera house" with live entertainment. Camping in a large grassy area is available within walking distance of all facilities (505-785-2291). All campsites have grills, restrooms, and showers on site. A larger range of motel options and prices exist only 16 miles further up the road in Carlsbad, the city.

Carlsbad Caverns are a series of eighty caves covering more than 73 square miles of labyrinths. Exploration continues to chart new caves. It is believed to be the largest such underground complex in the world. The main cavern is more than 30 miles long.

Self-guided tours range from easy to moderately difficult and typically take an hour or two or longer; ranger-guided tours can last all day. To get a taste, take the elevator down and stroll along one of the many well-lit trails

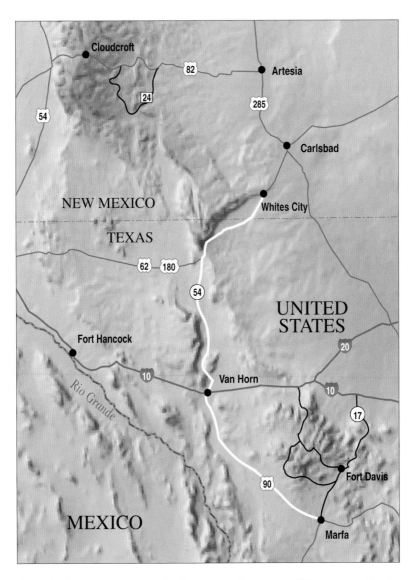

through the Great Room, which is more than two million square feet in size. There is even a snack bar and seating area down there! Every night at dusk during the summer, thousands of bats exit the caves for their nightly feeding. A viewing area provides "the best seat in the house" from which to watch them fly.

Day 8 Whites City to Cloudcroft, New Mexico

Distance *281 miles*
Features *This day starts in open desert and continues on to some absolutely knock-your-socks-off mountain roads and views.*

From Whites City continue north 22 miles on Hwy. 62/180 to Carlsbad. At the intersection with Hwy. 285 in Carlsbad, turn left toward Artesia. Between Carlsbad and Artesia you will notice a strong odor in the air created from the gasses associated with the production of crude oil. In Texas this is called the smell of money!

After approximately 34 miles, you will arrive in **Artesia.** Turn left (west) onto Hwy. 82 toward Cloudcroft. After 48 miles, turn left onto Hwy. 24 and continue 26 miles to the small town of **Pinion.** All these flat, straight roads through the high desert are reminiscent of the movie *High Plains Drifter.* From here, get ready for some superior mountain riding.

From Pinion, Hwy. 24 twists and climbs into the beautiful pine forests of the **Sacramento Mountains.** After roughly 22 miles, Hwy. 521 goes to the left into the town of **Weed.** If you want to meet some friendly people and have a good country lunch, try the **Weed Café** about two miles down Hwy. 521.

Texas grass

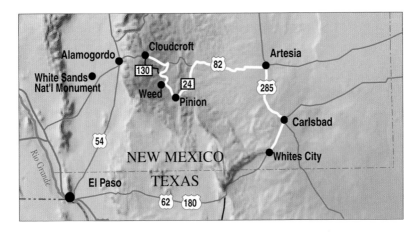

Two more miles down Hwy. 24, turn right onto Hwy. 130. Five miles later, turn left onto Hwy. 82. The 18 miles from here to Cloudcroft provide some of the finest motorcycle riding I have found. Whether you want some peg scraping or just enjoy wonderful mountain scenery, this is the road. Adjust your speed to suit your mood.

Cloudcroft (pop 600, elev. 8,950 ft.) was established when the **El Paso & Northeastern Railroad** built a spur from Alamagordo into the nearby Sacramento Mountains. Its purpose was to transport logs for railroad ties in their ambitious expansion northward. The spur, completed in 1900, showed the developers an area so beautiful that they decided to establish a resort for vacationers. Named Cloudcroft, a pasture for clouds, the resort was an instant success. Originally consisting of only a tent city, more permanent structures and private vacation homes were built gradually. Around 1947, when automobiles made railroads less profitable, the tracks were removed—but little has changed since then. Its population has remained relatively stable over the years and it offers all the services normally required by a visitor. An outdoor museum shows life as it was in the early years.

Located right on the square in the middle of town is *(Sandy's Choice)* the **Cloudcroft Hotel** (www.cloudcrofthotel.com, 505-682-3414, $110). The eight large nostalgic rooms have all amenities including clawfoot bath tubs and a resident ghost. Of the several dining options within walking distance, try the **Western Bar and Grill** for breakfast! Camping is available in US Forest Service campgrounds (575-682-7570) northeast of Cloudcroft on highway 244. There are five campgrounds within two miles of downtown, all with fire rings, toilet facilities, and water. Two campgrounds require a small amount of dirt riding on good maintained roads. They all offer a superb forested mountain setting.

Day 9   Cloudcroft to El Paso

Distance *106 miles*
Features *A thrilling descent of more than 4,300 feet in a short 16 miles
drops you back to the flat desert. Leaving the forests, you can see the
famous White Sands of New Mexico as you make a straightforward run to
El Paso.*

*Large rock
mountains seem
to just jump up
from the west
Texas desert.
(courtesy of
MotoDiscovery)*

From Cloudcroft continue west on Hwy. 82. The 16-mile, snaking descent to Alamagordo will have your heart pumping—but the views make it hard to keep your eyes on the road. From Alamagordo, you will be about 90 miles from El Paso on Hwy. 54. Signs to the El Paso airport as you approach the city are clear and frequent. This can also serve as a handy bypass to avoid the downtown area.

Side Trip

A visit to the **White Sands National Monument,** with its towering dunes of gypsum, can be quite a unique experience. The 16-mile scenic route has several well-marked pull-offs with interpretive signs explaining what you are seeing. Surrounded by the White Sands missile range, the park is sometimes closed for an hour or so when testing is in progress. To get there, turn right in Alamagordo onto Hwy. 70 (west). Fifteen miles later, you will see the park entrance and visitors' center on your right.

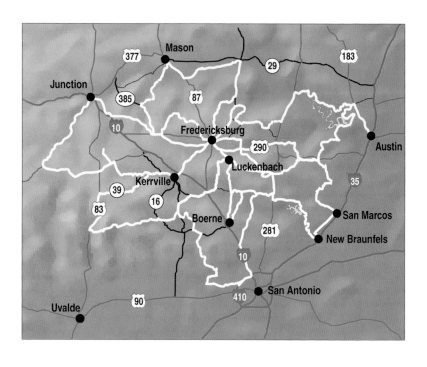

The Hill Country

The loosely defined area known as the Hill Country covers more than twenty thousand square miles of land atop the Balcones Escarpment in the "heart" of Texas. Although altitudes typically range only 1,500–1,700 ft., the dry air and summer temperatures that are relatively mild compared to the surrounding cities attract many visitors trying to escape the heat—and it offers all sorts of outdoor activities—including great motorcycling.

Located around Austin and San Antonio, the Hill Country is sprinkled with many small towns. Only a few of which can boast populations exceeding 10,000. Almost all government buildings and many homes and motels are built with the locally available pink limestone. Settled mostly by Europeans of German, Czech, and Polish descent, it retains much of that heritage to this day with many restaurants and cafés specializing in good food reflecting these roots.

The Hill Country presents a rider with endless options of up-and-down, curving, twisting roads. Many of which trail along rivers or atop high ridgelines with tremendous views of the countryside. When any roads in these routes are described as a "typical" Hill Country road, read this to mean that you are in for yet another fabulous motorcycle ride. After years, even locals report that they are still discovering superb new routes in this wonderfully interconnected "spaghetti bowl" of bike roads. DeLorme's *Texas Atlas & Gazetteer* has very detailed maps of the area and very helpful in navigating these smaller, less traveled roads.

The Hill Country can be quite hot in the summer—cool by Texas standards, of course, but still hot by most standards. During the mild winters, temperatures rarely fall below freezing at night and generally hover in the 60s or 70s during the day. The spring months of April and May carpet the Hill Country in bluebonnets, Indian paintbrush, and other wildflowers, to create a sight right out of a Monet painting.

This chapter outlines five one-day rides with a home base in **Fredericksburg,** and two days of riding to and from San Antonio to Fredericksburg via different routes. Please consider the rides outlined herein as only a brief introduction to what is available. I encourage you to allow some extra time for exploring the cities of San Antonio and Austin as well as finding some of the many "undiscovered" rides in this area.

In the hearts and minds of most Texans, the Alamo is one of the most sacred spots on this earth. (photo by Richard Reynolds/TxDOT)

SAN ANTONIO

San Antonio with a population exceeding 1.2 million constantly ranks as one of the ten best places to visit in the U.S. by travel magazines. *Conde Nast* has even rated it one of the top ten destinations in the world. San Antonio is the number one tourist draw in Texas. But don't think that you will be crowded among all the visitors. San Antonio is plenty big enough. Soon the laid-back, local, *mañana* pace will be rubbing off on you, and a good time will be had by all.

San Antonio's varied economy is grounded in the five U.S. military bases that exist in the city. The oldest, **Fort Sam Houston,** dates back to 1876. The federal government pours billions of dollars into the local economy in the form of paychecks for the troops and creates thousands of jobs to support their needs and desires. Tourism, the number two influence on the economy, funnels untold "outside" dollars through the local service industry. Bioscience and high-tech industries also thrive here, and there are eleven universities within the city limits. Being Texas, the oil business also contributes toward the growing and energetic economy.

As you would expect, San Antonio has many world-class museums and a multitude of cultural activities. The **San Antonio Convention and Visitors Bureau,** located at 317 Alamo Plaza (www.sanantoniocvb.com, 800-447-3372), is happy to direct you on the many interesting things to see and do here. They also have stands at the airport.

SAN ANTONIO ATTRACTIONS

A visit to the **Alamo** is a must, as is a stroll down the **Riverwalk** to have a delightful meal under the overhanging trees. The restaurants along this walk can provide any kind of food known in the world—except cheap food. A boat ride down the **San Antonio River** will let you survey the dining and shopping, while eyeballing the other tourists eyeballing you.

The **Alamo** (on Alamo Street between E. Houston and E. Crockett) is a former Spanish presidio that was constructed in 1724 and originally named the **Misión San Antonio de Valero**. It served as a home and workplace for the Spanish padres as they tried to convert the Indians. In 1793 the government took over the mission and expanded it into a true fort.

The Alamo is dear to the hearts of all Texans for the role it played in the fight for independence from Mexico in 1836. During the famous battle, 189 Texicans and other adventurers, most notably **Davy Crockett** and **Jim Bowie**, held off a Mexican army of more than 5,000 led by **General Santa Anna** for thirteen days before they were overrun and killed to the man. While the actual details of, and the motivation for, the battle remain fuzzy to this day, it is true that the delaying of the Mexican army at the Alamo allowed time for other Texicans to gather and form up into the military force

The San Antonio Riverwalk is a great place to shop, walk, or enjoy an excellent meal outdoors.

The Mission Trail in San Antonio offers you a chance to stop, learn some history, and explore the restored shrines.

that ultimately defeated the Mexicans at **San Jacinto.** It gave the Texicans their rallying battle cry, "Remember the Alamo!"

A self-guided walking tour is available throughout the complex and a 30-minute guided tour is given several times a day. Slide shows and a short film detail the story of the battle and the history of the site itself. There is ample parking near the Alamo, primarily in hotel parking garages.

These days, some controversy exists regarding the historical presentation of the battle, claiming it is too one-sided and does not fairly reflect the Mexican viewpoint. Be assured, you will leave with no doubts as to the Texican side of things!

As a side note, Texas law expressly forbids one from urinating on the Alamo. After being caught for a dastardly infraction, singer **Ozzy Osborne** has been permanently banned from performing in the state—Texas justice.

The **Riverwalk** is San Antonio's second most popular tourist attraction. You can enter the Riverwalk within two blocks of the Alamo and do not need to move your bike. Following the original path of the San Antonio River through downtown, The Riverwalk today is an entirely man-made stream constructed by the WPA in the late 1930s. With its cobbled walkways, overhanging trees, scores of outdoor dining options and, of course shopping, it is a pleasant stroll for locals and visitors alike. Although initially underutilized, underdeveloped and largely ignored, the area boomed in 1968 when the World's Fair (HemisFair) came to town. Massive construction to serve fair attendees along the river brought many businesses and hotels into the area. Today the Riverwalk is dotted with pleasant restaurants, shops, and major hotels. It is also safe. The city appreciates its value in tourist dollars and police presence is everywhere. Spend an hour or two strolling, take a boat ride and enjoy a meal along the Riverwalk.

In addition to the Alamo, the Spanish established four other missions along the San Antonio River in the 1700s: Missions Concepción, San José, San Juan, and Espada. At **San Antonio Missions National Historical Park** you can visit these missions, all of which still serve as active Catholic churches along the **Mission Trail**—an 8-mile ride clearly marked by Mission Trail signs. From the Alamo, go south on S. Alamo, pick up trail signs, and go left onto South St. Mary's Street. Each of the missions has a unique history and varies greatly in size and style. If you only have time to visit one, I recommend the **Mission San José,** which also serves as park headquarters and offers a free film that outlines the history of the missions and the Indian tribes who built them.

SAN ANTONIO LODGING

San Antonio offers lodgings in every price range and category. The airport area has hotels and motels from about every chain known to man. The downtown area has a nice selection of mostly upscale accommodations. If you want a real treat, and your budget can handle it, try *(Sandy's Choice)* the **Menger Hotel** (www.mengerhotel.com, 800-292-1050, $225). It is literally "in the shade" of the Alamo. Originally built in 1859, the hotel has been constantly renovated and updated through the years, yet maintains its original look. The staff and owners, well aware of the hotel's historical significance, are constantly on the lookout for any encroachment on its appearance.

The closest campground to downtown is the **Dixie Kampground,** located at 1011 Gembler Road (210-337-6502; 800-759-5627, $20). Three miles east of downtown off I-35, take the Coliseum Exit and go south one half-mile to Gembler and follow signs. They have nice shaded camping sites with all facilities and a camp store. Ask about buses into town if you'd rather not worry about navigating and parking your bike.

Day 1   San Antonio to Fredericksburg

Distance *125 miles*

Features *This short ride will get you out of the traffic of the big city and give you an introduction to Hill Country riding. Fredericksburg makes a great home base for the next four loops. Please do not be fooled by the low mileage; a good bit of this day consists of very slow speed roads.*

From the intersection of I-10 and Loop 410 on the northwest side of San Antonio (near the airport), take 410 W for approximately 11 miles and then take the Hwy. 3487 Exit (Culbera Road). After a mile or so on this frontage road, take a right onto the actual highway at the first traffic signal. A block later, turn left onto Hwy. 1957.

After you cross the intersection with Loop 1604, Hwy. 1957 becomes two-lane and you will have exited the city. Eight miles after leaving the interstate you will come to a T-intersection with Hwy. 471; take a right and go 10 miles, then take a left onto Hwy. 1283. Hwy. 471 runs through flat farming land, but for some reason, the road has several 90-degree turns—not all marked—although you will have excellent visibility through the turns.

Fall colors in the hill country really add to your riding pleasure.

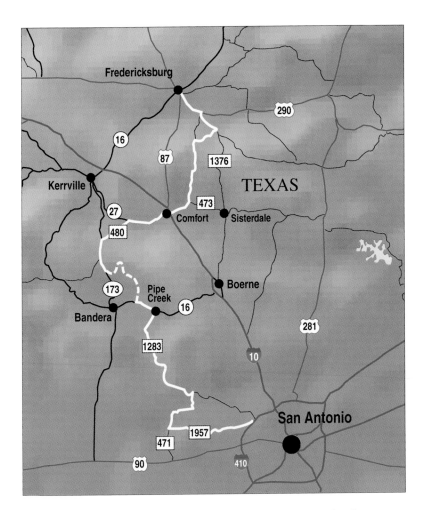

Welcome to the Hill Country! As you follow Hwy. 1283 for the next 22 miles to the intersection with Hwy. 16 in Pipe Creek you will get an idea of what is ahead of you on the trip. In spite of the high-speed designation of the road before you, you will get some wonderful views as you top hill after hill, and twist through the curves.

At the T-intersection with Hwy. 16 in the town of Pipe Creek, turn left, continue for approximately four miles, and turn right onto Privilege Creek Road. After two miles, the road turns to good, hard-packed dirt for about eight miles. Go left at the first Y-intersection onto Old School Road, toward Polly's Chapel. As you run along the river with cliffs on either side, note that the speed limit for this stretch is posted as 30 mph, but I do not recommend going this fast on most of the road.

Side Trip to Polly's Chapel

Shortly after taking the turn onto Old School Road, you pass over a cattle guard and a right turn takes off toward **Polly's Chapel,** maybe a quarter of a mile away. Sitting out by itself on a small hill surrounded by live oak trees, Polly's Chapel was built by hand out of native stone in 1882 by **Policarpo Rodriguez,** a former Texas Ranger, army scout, and guide. It was here that he converted to the Methodist religion and services are still being held there today.

I recommend you take this small side trip, but note that there are about 20 yards of this road that require caution on a street bike. After visiting Polly's Chapel, return the short distance to the main road and turn right.

Continue on Old School Road for approximately three miles until you come to a Y-intersection, where you will bear left. After another two miles, you come to another Y-intersection. Take the right hand fork. In just two more miles, the road Ts into pavement, where you will turn right. You soon come to another Y-intersection; take the right fork. In two more miles, at an

Named after its builder, Polly's Chapel sits alone in a remote area. Services are still held here.

intersection with a yield sign, proceed straight ahead. Six miles later you will be at a T-intersection, where you will turn right onto Hwy. 173.

By now you have probably experienced your first time of getting lost in the Hill Country and you understand why I called it a "spaghetti bowl" of great riding roads at the beginning of this chapter.

Alternate Route

Should you not wish to ride this short dirt stretch or try to navigate through the area, don't take the turn off Hwy. 16 on to Privilege Creek Road after Pipe Creek, but stay on Hwy. 16 into Bandera where you can turn right on to Hwy. 173. The dirt route, however, is a delightful ride and I highly recommend that you try it.

After about seven miles of good, high-speed riding on Hwy. 173, turn right onto Hwy. 480. Another seven miles will get you to the intersection with Hwy. 27, where you should turn right again, and after nine miles you will come into the small town of Comfort.

From Comfort you have two options for reaching Fredericksburg. The most direct and fastest route is to turn left onto Hwy. 87, and after approximately 23 miles of good road, you will be there. Your other choice is somewhat longer, consists of much better riding roads, and is more fun. To take this option, turn left onto Hwy. 473 in Comfort and head toward Sisterdale. After five miles, Hwy. 473 bears off to the right; stay left and follow signs indicating the **Old Tunnel Wildlife Management Area.** This ride is an absolute delight and has some serious curves on it that are not always clearly marked. Take extra care and enjoy! The Old Tunnel Wildlife Management Area was created to protect the many animals that live here. From June through October, the old railroad tunnel is home to more than a million bats and their departure at sunset is an amazing sight.

Fourteen miles after leaving Hwy. 473, turn right onto Luckenbach-Cane City Road. Be alert. This turn is only marked by a very small sign. After two miles, turn left onto Hwy. 1376, go five miles, and turn left at the T-intersection with Hwy. 290. Nine miles later you will arrive in Fredericksburg.

Fredericksburg, (pop. 8,000) is considered by many to be the center of the Hill Country. People flock here year 'round on day trips from San Antonio and Austin or for overnight stays during the spring when the wildflowers are in bloom. It can become crowded on weekends during this time and, if possible, plan your visit for weekdays.

A visit to this roadhouse in Fredericksburg is almost a "must" for some riders.

Settled by German immigrants in 1846, Fredericksburg wears its heritage proudly. German is still the primary language of many residents, and the downtown architecture also pays homage to its roots. Fredericksburg also holds a unique footnote in history: its original German settlers entered into a treaty with the local **Comanche Indians** that was never broken, the only such treaty between white men and Native Americans to hold such a distinction. Fredericksburg was also the birthplace of **Admiral Chester Nimitz,** and a very good museum covering World War II in the Pacific and the life of the Admiral is located at 328 E. Main St, in a building that was the site of the old Nimitz Hotel. There are several rooms restored to that era for viewing. Ask at the front desk about the current times and starting locations for walking tours of the town.

The number one place to stay *(Sandy's Choice)* is the **Sunday House Inn** located at 501 E. Main Street (www.sundayhouse.com, 830-997-4484, $100). It includes a free breakfast coupon redeemable at the **Sunday House Restaurant** next door. Another choice is the **Dietzel Motel** (www.dietzelmotel.com, 830-997-3330, $75), located about one mile west of downtown on Hwy. 290, just after Hwy. 87 goes to the right. This place right out of the 50s is perfectly adequate. Next door is **Friedhelm's Bavärian**

Restaurant and Bar and the ever popular **Skookers Roadhouse**, a local biker hangout, is just around the corner on Hwy. 87. If you are a B&B person, this is the place, as the town seems to have an almost endless supply. To reserve a room in a B&B call **Bed and Breakfast of Fredericksburg** at 830-997-4712. Campers can set up along the Pedernales River at the **Lady Bird Johnson Municipal Park** ($10) just south of town.

The problem with the food in Fredericksburg is that there are so many good places to eat it is hard to choose. Most tourists leave a few pounds heavier after their visit. German cuisine is the focus at **Das Lindenbaum** (with attached *biergarten)* at 312 E. Main and **Friedhelm's Bavärian Restaurant and Bar** at 905 W. Main. Great southwestern and Cajun dishes are served at the **Navajo Grill** at 209 E. Main, and the all-around pub menu at the **Fredericksburg Brewing Co.** at 245 E. Main has something for everyone. Of the many good German pastry shops in town, try **Dietz Bakery** at 218 E. Main or the **Fredericksburg Bakery,** at 141 E. Main Street.

People come to the hill country to picnic, camp, and enjoy a swim.

Loop 1 Fredericksburg to Austin

Distance *225 miles*
Features *This ride contains two of the most talked-about roads in the Hill Country: Willow City Loop and Lime Creek Road. Visit the historic city of Austin and the LBJ ranch, and check out the views of the massive lake system north of Austin.*

In Fredericksburg take Hwy. 16 north for 20 miles and make a right turn onto Willow City Loop Road. Please note that this is past the right turn on Hwy. 1323 to Willow City. Highway 16 is a good high-speed road with a fair amount of traffic for the Hill Country. Willow City Loop Road is one of the many one-lane, two-way roads you will find in this area, and it bounces up and down, twisting and turning through the countryside for all of its 13 miles. You should stay alert for oncoming traffic, keep a sharp eye for live-stock out on the open range, and look for sand or gravel washes in the dips. Slow down and enjoy the ride.

As you come through Willow City, proceed straight ahead at the intersection with Rural Road 1323. After 18 miles of some of the best riding to be found anywhere, you will arrive in the one-store town of **Sandy**. Be extra careful along this stretch as it does have some extreme dips and a few tight curves that can sneak up on you if you are not paying attention. Clearing through the traffic and congestion of Sandy, take the first paved left onto Sandy/Round Mountain Road, which quickly turns to good hard-packed dirt for eight miles through the countryside before intersecting with Hwy. 281 just north of Johnson City.

Alternate Route

If you do not wish to ride the dirt section, continue on Rural Road 1323 until it intersects with Hwy. 281 where you turn left toward Marble Falls. About 13 miles from Marble Falls, you rejoin the recommended route.

At the end of the Sandy/Round Mountain Road turn left at the T-intersection with Hwy. 281. Thirteen good, high-speed miles later you will cross the river and enter the town of **Marble Falls**. At the top of the hill on your right is the **Bluebonnet Café**, famous for its down-home cooking and desserts. Try to arrive hungry!

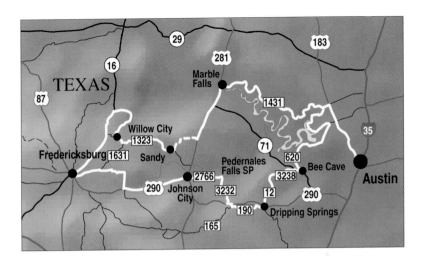

In Marble Falls, take a right onto Rural Road 1431. Go 39 miles and turn right onto Lime Creek Road, a stretch that passes through several small towns and offers magnificent views of the rivers and lakes that make up this part of the Hill Country. As you approach the outskirts of Austin, the road becomes a four-laner.

Side Trip to Austin

Austin once served as the national capitol of the Republic of Texas; it was demoted to a mere state capitol when Texas joined the Union. Should you wish to visit this delightful city, continue on Hwy. 1431 past the Lime Creek Road turnoff to the T-intersection with Hwy. 183, where you should take a right. Follow Hwy. 183 to the intersection with I-35 and go south.

You will find hotels to fit every taste and budget along this route. For a real treat, try staying at *(Sandy's Choice)* the **Driskill Hotel** (www.driskillhotel.com, 800-252-9367, $400+) located at 604 Brazos Street. Constructed in 1886, the building served as a meeting place for the Texas government until the capitol was completed. Built to the highest standards of the day, the hotel retains its original décor while having all the modern amenities.

Austin (metro area pop. 1,600,000+) has been picked as one of the top five places to live in the United States by both *Money* and *Fortune* magazines. The government of Texas and its employees form a large part of the city. The more than 50,000 students of the

The Governor's Mansion in Austin reflects the influence of the South in Texas. (photo by Gay Shackelford/ TxDOT)

University of Texas also make up a large part of the local culture. And lastly, the electronics industry has contributed to the city's economic health: today, Austin is the home of Texas Instruments, Dell Computer, IBM, Hewlett-Packard, Apple Computer, and more than 200 other high-tech companies, and is often referred to as the **Silicon Valley of the East.** As a result of the above, the people of Austin are the most highly educated of any city in the United States, with one-third holding college degrees.

In addition, Austin is a major record recording center to rival Nashville with its country music and Memphis with its blues. Whatever your taste in music, you'll have your choice of nightclubs with live entertainment every night of the week. While Austin is a major city with museums, art galleries, and cultural opportunities to match any other major city in the world, it does have some unique sites of its own.

The **state capitol building,** completed in 1888, is the largest state capitol in the nation and is even seven feet taller than the U.S. Capitol in Washington, D.C. Its exterior consists of pink limestone mined at Marble Falls only a few miles away. The more than eight acres of interior floor space are covered with a copper dome that is topped by a statue of the Goddess of Liberty. The rotunda, which houses the original **Texas Declaration of Independence** and the **Ordinance of Secession,** has a terrazzo floor featuring the flags of the six nations that have, at one time or another, claimed dominion over Texas: Spain, France, Mexico, the Republic of

Texas, the Confederate States of America and the United States. Take a free, guided tour that includes the governor's offices and the chambers of the state senate and the house of representatives—just brace yourself to be bombarded by "Texas-sized" statistics!

By itself, the **Congress Avenue Bridge** is not much of an attraction, but during the summer, an estimated 1.5 million Mexican bats call the place "home." The bats migrate and nest here from May through October, and their daily sunset exodus into the night sky is an amazing sight. Volunteers from **Bat Conservation International** are on duty to answer questions, or you can call the bat hotline (512-416-5700, ext. 3636) for information.

Austin is the center of the fourteen statewide campuses that make up the vast **University of Texas** system, which consistently ranks among the top ten schools in the nation. Sitting on a 357-acre site in downtown Austin, UTexas is the home of more than 50,000 students; it is so large, one residence hall has its own zip code. The university library is the sixth-largest in the country, with more than six million volumes. The endowment of the University of Texas is one of the largest in the world, due to the fact that the state legislature gave the school more than two million acres of land in the west Texas desert, which were later discovered to contain vast oilfields. (It's no coincidence that the Petroleum Engineering Dept. is world class!)

There are several museums on the campus, but the most popular tourist spot is the **UT Tower** from which, in August 1966, **Charles Whitman** shot and killed 15 people and wounded 33 more before being shot to death himself. The second most visited spot is the **Lyndon B. Johnson Library and Museum** which contains four floors of memorabilia and a replica of the Oval Office during his terms as president.

For everything you ever wanted to know about Texas history, visit the state-of-the-art **Bob Bullock Texas State History Museum**, located at the corner of MLK Blvd. and Congress Avenue. Don't miss the **Texas Spirit Theater** showing of the film *Star of Destiny*, a Hollywood-class production that will have you charging into the streets screaming, "Remember the Alamo!" Plan to spend at least a half day here, enjoying the hands-on, interactive exhibits. Underground parking is available.

Lime Creek Road runs for 11 miles along the lake, and it appears no attempts were made to grade or straighten when it was built, as it clings to the hillsides and meanders along. At the STOP sign turn left onto Rural Road 2769, go seven miles, and make a right turn onto Hwy. 620, which runs along the lakefront where there are many gated communities of million-dollar homes. This road also has several very sharp curves with recommended speeds of 15 to 25 mph. Believe the signs!

After 18 miles on Hwy. 620, turn right on Hwy. 71 in Bee Cave; three miles later, take a left onto Rural Road 3238. After five miles, turn left onto Hwy. 12 toward Dripping Springs. You will have left behind the build-up suburbia surrounding Austin, as Hwy. 12 runs along a ridgeline almost its entire length. After five miles, turn right onto Hwy. 290, and follow the four-lane main road for only a short distance, maybe two blocks, and take a left onto Hwy. 190 (Creek Road). It is easy to miss this turn; the road is directly across from the signs indicating Loop 64 off to the right.

Creek Road soon becomes a one-lane, two-way road, with several one-lane bridges along its nine-mile path. Three miles after the turnoff from Hwy. 290, turn right at the intersection with County Road 220 to continue on Creek Road. At the T-intersection with Hwy. 165, turn right, and then at the T-intersection with Hwy. 290, take another left.

In approximately three miles, turn right onto Rural Road 3232 and proceed another seven miles to the T-intersection with Rural Road 2766. Take a right, and then an almost immediate left at the signs denoting the entranceway into the **Pedernales Falls State Park.** As you might guess by the name, the park adjoins the **Pedernales River** and has a view of the falls. In the summer, this is a popular spot to launch canoes for a pristine paddle in the wilderness.

After visiting the park, return to Rural Road 2766 and turn right. Continue on this road for 12 miles and then turn right on Hwy. 290. After completing the run on Rural Road 2766, you may begin to wonder just how many excellent motorcycle roads exist in the Hill Country. Too many to count. Enjoy!

You are now in Johnson City and after only a short block or so Hwy. 290 turns left; take this turn. As you leave Johnson City the high-speed, four-lane highway is elevated and affords overwhelming views. Fifteen miles later, the LBJ Ranch will be on your right. Officially known as the **Lyndon B. Johnson State and National Historical Parks,** the complex contains the ranch house that served as the "Texas Whitehouse" during Johnson's term as president, a reconstructed cabin which represents his boyhood home, an active visitors' center detailing his life and accomplishments, and the family

Texans are proud of their heritage as shown by this sculpture in front of the Bob Bulick Museum of Texas History in Austin.

graveyard where he is buried. A 90-minute guided bus tour points out the sights and explains what you are seeing. Note that this is no place for trotting out political opinions detrimental to the memory of the 36th president. To Texans, Johnson is still considered as almost a God.

After your visit to the ranch complex, exit and continue on Hwy. 290 for about a mile and make a right turn on Rural Road 1623. After four miles take a left onto 2721, proceed to the intersection with Rural Road 1631, and go straight ahead. Thirteen miles later, turn right onto Hwy. 290 to downtown Fredericksburg.

Loop 2 Fredericksburg to Mason

Distance *165 miles*

Features *This ride affords a visit to Enchanted Rock State Park, a "must-stop" at Cooper's Bar-B-Q in Mason, opportunities to view exotic game, and a short dual-sport ride that includes three stream crossings.*

Start at the intersection of Hwy. 290/87 and Hwy. 16 in downtown Fredericksburg. Go north on Hwy. 290/87 for a few blocks. Make a right turn onto Rural Road 965 to begin another day of delightful Hill Country riding. After 17 miles, Enchanted Rock State Park will be on your left.

Enchanted Rock, a popular spot with rock climbers, juts up 325 ft. and covers more than 70 acres. The night air is filled with strange creaking and groaning sounds due to the contraction of the rocks as they cool each day. The Indians thought the place was haunted and it is believed they performed human sacrifices here to appease the gods. Even today, many people consider it a spiritual power point on Earth. You can ride down a short loop to get a closer view and take the obligatory picture of your bike in front of this amazing rock. A small welcome center has exhibits explaining more details.

Enchanted Rock rises 325 feet above the surrounding terrain.

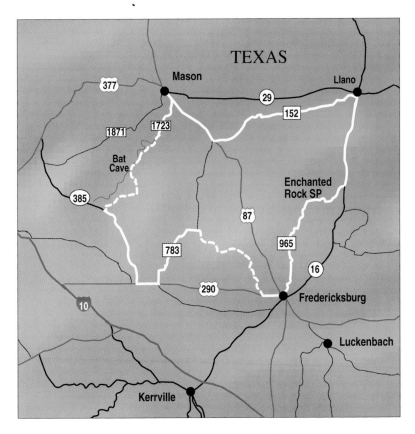

Following your visit, continue northward on Rural Road 965 for nine miles. At the intersection with Hwy. 16, turn left toward Llano. After 15 miles of good, high-speed road make a left turn onto Hwy. 152. If you cross the bridge going into Llano you will have gone too far.

Hwy. 152 runs 20 miles until it intersects with Hwy. 87—and it is some of the best the Hill Country has to offer. Nine miles into this stretch, be on the lookout as the route takes a left turn just before the small town of Castell. Rather than scraping your pegs (which can easily be done), I suggest you slow down and savor this wonderful ride; there are several curves with recommended speed limits in the 15–20 mph range.

At the intersection with Hwy. 87, turn right toward Mason. After 11 miles on this major highway, turn left onto Rural Road 1723 (Jamestown Bat Cave Road).

Side Trip

For a real Texas treat, continue into **Mason** just a few short blocks and let your nose lead you to **Cooper's Bar-B-Q.** You'll see the smoke rising before you actually see the building. Once you've sorted out all the delicious smells, proceed to the outdoor pits where all sorts of meat is cooked and choose the size and nature of your carnivorous feast. Your selection will be cut and placed on a piece of white waxed paper that will serve as your plate. From there, you go inside to have your order weighed and to stock up on sides of cold slaw, beans, and potato salad. Then, have a seat and pig out. Afterward, backtrack on Hwy. 16 for a mile or so and make a right turn onto Hwy. 1723.

Ten miles after turning onto Rural Road 1723, the road turns to dirt, and the next 18-mile stretch includes three places where you have to ford the **James River.** It is very do-able and fun on a dual-sport bike, but I don't think it would be much fun on a heavy dresser.

Alternate Route

If you decide to skip the dirt, continue through Mason and take a left onto Rural Road 1871. At the T-intersection with Hwy. 385, turn left and pick up the remainder of the route after passing E. Mill Road. This will add a few miles, but is quicker than the suggested route.

As you travel the 28 miles of road from Hwy. 87 to the intersection with Hwy. 385, you will really be in the backcountry. Keep your eyes peeled for wild turkey and deer. Those stretches of high fencing you see often seal-off exotic animal ranches with species imported from around the world.

Two miles after leaving State Hwy. 87, turn right onto Rural Road 2389, which turns to good, hard-packed dirt after another 8 miles. There are several intersections on the 10-mile paved stretch that can be confusing; just follow the signs to the bat cave. This road runs right along the banks of the James River and should not be missed. Two miles after starting on the dirt, a paved road takes off to the right to a privately owned ranch; continue straight on the dirt. After 6 miles of dirt, you will come to the first of three water crossings along this road.

The first crossing is by far the longest and deepest (perhaps one-hundred yards of foot-deep water. Before starting across, note the barbed wire fence on the left: if the water is up to the lower strand, it's about 12 inches deep. The next two crossings are much shorter and only have an inch or two of water in them.

Shortly after passing the bat cave, make a right turn onto E. Mill Road. Another seven miles of dirt will bring you to the T-intersection with Hwy. 385, where you turn left. Follow Hwy. 385 for 14 miles to the T-intersection with Hwy. 290. This ride is fairly straight with lots of gentle ups and downs. There are several exotic game ranches along this road, too.

Turn left onto Hwy. 290, go three miles, and turn left on Hwy. 783, which goes through a more settled area with farms and pastures on each side. Don't let this road lull you into a false sense of security, as there are several sharp curves that can sneak up on you. Fourteen miles later, turn right onto Doss Spring Creek Road, go a short two miles, and turn left onto Crenwelge Ridge Road. Six miles later, turn left onto Rehwienheiner Road, and proceed six miles to the T-intersection with Hwy. 290. The 24-mile loop from the time you leave Hwy. 290 until your return has a good many sections of one-lane, two-way traffic and lots of open range. It is a beautiful Hill Country ride; slow down and enjoy.

Turn left on Hwy. 290 and about nine miles later you will be back in Fredericksburg.

While lacking in amenities, Cooper's Bar-B-Q in Mason does serve up some real Texas cooking.

Loop 3 Guadalupe Fork Road and Luckenbach

Distance *195 miles*

Features *The Lower Guadalupe Fork Road is one of the best and longest rides in the Hill Country. Visit the Cowboy Artists of America Museum in Kerrville and "gang up" with local riders.*

Starting at the intersection of Hwys. 290 and 16 in Fredericksburg, take Hwy. 16 south toward Kerrville. After 25 miles of good, high-speed road you will go under the interstate and enter Kerrville, with a very complete welcome center on your right, just across from the EconoLodge.

    Kerrville (pop. 20,000) is a popular Hill Country getaway for hot city folks living in Austin and San Antonio. Tourism is the primary industry, and outdoor lovers flock here to ride horses, hike, and enjoy nature. The old downtown area has been restored to its original glory and now blooms with shops and sidewalk restaurants. To see the historical district turn left one block beyond the intersection of Hwys. 16 and 27.

Beer drinking and guitar picking are major activities in Luckenbach.
(photo by John Neff)

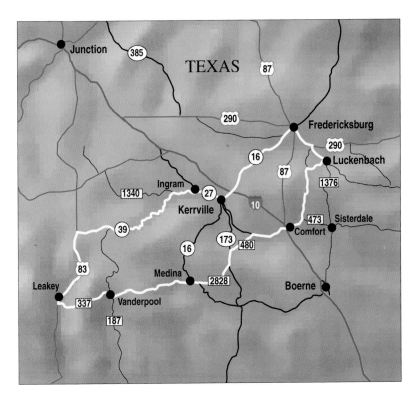

To get to the **Cowboy Artists of America Museum,** continue down Hwy. 16, cross the river, and turn left onto Hwy. 173. A half-mile later it will be on your right. The museum features historically accurate paintings and sculptures depicting the cowboy and his life. You will come away with a view that is very different from Hollywood's portrayal. After your visit to the museum, backtrack to the intersection with Hwy. 27 and turn left.

If you do not wish to visit the museum, at the intersection of Hwys. 16 and 27 turn right onto Hwy. 27 toward Ingram. After six miles of four-lane road, you will come to an intersection; go straight ahead to get onto Hwy. 39 (Lower Guadalupe Fork Rd). For the next 41 miles, the road runs along the banks of the **Guadalupe River,** following its turns through rocky, wooded country. You will cross the river a half-dozen times. The speed limit on this road is typically 50 mph, but the road flattens and straightens out the last 10 miles or so and the speed limit increases to 70 mph.

At the T-intersection with Hwy. 83, turn left toward Leakey. While this is a major highway, it does offer a stunning panoramic view of the country-side. There is a super pull-off about 10 miles down this road which is perfect for getting a shot of your noble beast in the Hill Country. Nine miles later

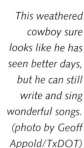
This weathered cowboy sure looks like he has seen better days, but he can still write and sing wonderful songs. (photo by Geoff Appold/TxDOT)

on Hwy. 83, you will arrive in **Leakey.** For good country cooking and local gossip, try the **Frio Canyon Café.**

Continue south on Hwy. 83 for approximately one mile and make a left turn on Hwy. 337 toward Vanderpool. Again, this 17-mile stretch of Hill Country road will have you grinning from ear-to-ear and begging for more. As you approach Vanderpool, Hwy. 337 makes a 90-degree right as it joins with Hwy. 187, and then turns left just a short distance down the road; both turns are clearly marked.

Continue on Hwy. 337 for 18 miles. When you reach Hwy. 16 in Medina, turn right and go three miles. Turn left onto Rural Road 2828,

Willie Nelson

If any one person can be credited with the popularity and evolution of country music since the 1970s, it would be Willie Nelson. Born in Abbott, Texas, on April 30, 1933, Nelson displayed his musical talent early in life, making his first musical performance at the age of 10 years, playing with a polka band. In 1961 he moved to Nashville, Tennessee, to start a career in country music. Although he was successful in writing several songs that became huge hits and country standards, they were originally recorded by other, better-known singers. The industry discouraged Nelson from becoming a singer himself, on the belief that his voice was not good enough nor his style traditional enough to be successful.

In 1970, Willie returned to his native Texas and began recording in Austin. The public flocked to the new sound and a string of number one hits soon followed. Nelson's appearance on stage, the content of his songs, and his decision to record in Austin instead of Nashville soon branded him an "outlaw." Other performers followed suit, however, and Austin has grown into a major recording city for all types of music. Today, with more than 200 records selling over a million copies each, Willie Nelson has proven his talent beyond all doubts. He was inducted into the Country Music Hall of Fame in 1993, and has even starred in several hit movies.

But life has not always been good to Willie Nelson. He has suffered from bad marketing, and his troubles with the IRS are well known. His reputation as an avid pot smoker was confirmed when he was convicted for possession of cannabis. And, he has experienced many highly publicized personal problems along the way. These difficulties only made his fans love him more.

Today, making his home in the Texas Hill Country, Willie Nelson continues to perform around the world. He is the founder and primary force behind Farm Aid, and even has become a major spokesman for the Texas Department of Tourism, appearing in their commercials and inviting people "to come on down and visit Texas."   ✪

proceed nine miles, and turn left onto Hwy. 173. After 3 miles, turn right on Hwy. 480. Six miles later, at the intersection of Hwy. 27, turn right toward **Comfort**. This is a nice town with a historical district that is perfect for an interesting stroll or afternoon coffee-and-pastry break.

The combined post office, general store, and bar in Luckenbach offers an amazingly wide variety of items for sale. (photo by John Neff)

In Comfort, take a left turn onto Hwy. 473 toward Sisterdale, and follow the road signs to get through several intersections (just keep going straight). After five miles, Hwy. 473 will bear off to the right; go straight ahead following the signs indicating the Old Tunnel Wildlife Management Area. Local bikers know this as the **"Grapetown Rd.,"** and it has some serious curves, not all of which are marked. It's an absolute delight.

The **Old Tunnel Wildlife Management Area** was created to protect the many animals that inhabit the area. From June through October, the old railroad tunnel is home to more than one million bats and their departure at sunset is an amazing sight; the show is even better with a full moon.

Fourteen miles after leaving Hwy. 473, turn right onto Luckenbach-Cane City Road. Be alert, as this turn is marked only by a very small sign. After two miles, turn right onto Hwy. 1376. Two miles farther, you will see the right turn into **Luckenbach**. If you cross the bridge, you have gone too far.

Founded as a German community in the 1800s, the entire town of Luckenbach (pop. 10) was purchased by **Hondo Crouch** in the 1970s. The late Crouch, whose bust now sits in front of the general store, used to invite his friends to stop by to play music, toss horseshoes and washers, tell jokes and stories, and just generally have a good ol' time. The rest of the world learned of Luckenbach when Willie Nelson and Waylon Jennings sang, "... in Luckenbach, Texas, ain't nobody feeling no pain ..." and the town has become a mecca for country music fans.

The **Luckenbach General Store** also serves as a post office, souvenir shop, and bar. On weekends, shady picnic tables in back of the store provide a great setting for drinking Lone Star beer from long neck bottles, swapping lies, and listening to amateur guitar pickers plying their hobby. The old dance hall occasionally hosts name entertainers. It's a favorite Sunday afternoon destination for hundreds of bikers. Saturday is good too, but Sunday seems to be the big day. Should you visit Luckenbach on a Wednesday, you will find the whole town closed.

The ten acres that make up Luckenbach can even be rented for private events! Among the more infamous are the **Hell Hath No Fury Ladies State Chili Championship** (first Saturday in October), Texas Independence Celebration (March), and **Luckenbach's 4th of July Picnic** (sometimes hosted by Willie Nelson). For more info, surf over to www.luckenbachtexas.com.

After visiting Luckenbach, return to Hwy. 1376, and turn left. Five miles will take you to the intersection with Hwy. 290. You are now only one left turn and nine miles from completing your day as you return to Fredericksburg.

Luckenbach residents are proud of their modern communication facilities.

Loop 4 Wilkommen au Deutschland

Distance *238 miles*

Features *This ride has more high-speed roads than the other loops. Couple that with a truly unique biker hangout in Canyon City, the always-popular River Road ride, and a visit to the oldest Dance Hall in Texas, and you have a lot in store. If you still haven't had enough, you can visit the larger Hill Country towns of New Bruanfels and San Marcos.*

From the intersection of Hwys. 290 and 16 in downtown Fredericksburg, take Hwy. 290 east for six miles, and turn right on Hwy. 1376. The twenty-eight mile ride to the intersection with Hwy. 87 just outside Boerne is, again, a typical Hill Country road that can be ridden at good speed. Turn left onto Hwy. 87 and in a mile and a half you will be at the Boerne town square. Turn left at the Exxon station onto Hwy. 474.

    Boerne is another Hill Country town founded by German immigrants in the 1840s. Today, it has become quite an artists' colony and abounds with galleries and antique stores. A town of approximately 9,000 people, Boerne has more than 140 buildings dating back to its founding days. There seems to be a festival of some sort nearly every weekend. The **Boerne**

The oldest continuous German music band in the United States continues to perform on warm summer evenings in Boerne, Texas, and around the world.

Village Band, the oldest German band in the U.S., travels all over the world performing Teutonic music specialties. On summer evenings, they hold a concert series known as the **Abendkonzerte** in the town's main plaza.

After 18 miles, Hwy. 474 intersects with Hwy. 473; turn right and go 14 miles to the intersection with Hwy. 281. This 32-mile ride on Hwys. 474 and 473 are fairly typical Hill Country roads that can be ridden at fairly high speeds. Towards the end of this section, a few well-marked, sharp curves will require you to slow down.

Turn right onto Hwy. 281, go three miles, and then turn left onto Hwy. 306. After 18 miles of delightful riding, turn right onto Hwy. 2673 in Canyon City. If you look to your left at this intersection, you will see **The Shanty,** with, as the sign says, "Drinking and Dancing." It's a popular destination for weekend motorcyclists looking to take long neck beers out back and sit along the banks of the river under the shade of 100-year-old oak trees. If it happens to be open when you go by, stop in and peruse the collection of bras dangling from the rafters, discarded by patrons as the joint "heats up." The skid marks on the dance floor were made by bikers who decided to "cut the rug" with their machines instead of their feet!

If you like good, authentic German food served by beautiful waitresses, you will have endless options in the Hill Country. (courtesy of TxDOT)

After only two miles on Hwy. 2673, turn left at the traffic signal in Sattler onto **River Road**. This road has earned its designation as one of the most famous in the hill country, as it follows the **Guadalupe River** overhung with towering trees and stone cliffs. The speed limit is only 20 mph and you are well advised to obey it. Eleven miles later at the T-intersection turn left to stay with River Road, proceed two more miles, and take a left turn onto Loop 337 just outside New Braunsfels.

Side Trip

The first exit off Loop 337 (turn left after exiting) offers you the opportunity to visit the historic town of **Gruene**. It has been carefully restored and contains the oldest dance hall in Texas, where country greats, such as **George Strait, Bo Diddley, The Dixie Chicks, Jerry Lee Lewis, Garth Brooks,** and **Willie Nelson** have performed. The hall was also used as a set in the movie *Michael*, starring **John Travolta**.

Continue down Loop 337 until you intersect with I-35 Business. At this intersection, turn left. If you wish to visit downtown New Braunsfels, turn right here.

New Braunsfels sits at the intersection of the Comal and Guadalupe Rivers. With a population approaching 35,000, it is the second largest city

Texas Wine

Franciscan padres planted the first grapevines in Texas in 1662, nearly a century before cultivation started in California. The weather and soil conditions in certain parts of the state are almost perfect for growing grapes and, until Prohibition, Texas led the nation in wine production. Today, Texas ranks fifth among wine producing states, and it markets many of its wares to France. The Hill Country alone has more than 16 wineries where you are welcome to drop in for free tours and daily tastings.

Most Texas wines are varietals; that is, they are made almost entirely from the type of grape listed on the bottle. The cabernet sauvignon, merlot, chardonnay, and pinot noir are considered the best and are the most popular. These fine wines are often proudly referred to as "Chateau de Bubba" and "Vin de Lone Star." For more information, call the Texas Department of Agriculture (512-463-7624) and request their free brochure, *Texas Wine Country Tour Guide*.   ✪

in the Hill Country. Just another one of the many towns and cities that have grown from the German settlements of the 1840s, today New Braunsfels honors these roots with good German food and architecture. The annual **Wurstfest** in November features local sausages and German bands in traditional garb. Of special interest to the biker is the **Alamo Classic Car Museum** located on I-35 between Exits 180 and 182. The huge facility houses more than 150 restored antique automobiles, motorcycles, and fire trucks. If it is time to eat, try **Krause's Café** at 148 S. Castell for some local German favorites.

I-35 Business runs beside the actual interstate for a mile or two before intersecting with Hwy. 306, where you need to make a left turn. In addition to the **New Braunsfels Visitors' Center,** you will find a couple of motorcycle dealerships along this short stretch, should you need to have your bike serviced.

After one mile on Hwy. 306, turn right onto Hwy. 1102 for a fairly straight, flat seven miles to the intersection with Hwy. 2439; go straight ahead onto Hwy. 2439. After 11 miles, turn left onto Hwy. 12.

Side Trip

If you want to visit downtown **San Marcos,** just go straight ahead at the previous intersection. In a few short blocks you will be in the town square. San Marcos, with a population approaching 40,000, is located on the eastern edge of the Hill Country on the **San Marcos River.** Although it was named by the Spanish, who found it on St. Marks Day, they were never successful in establishing themselves here. It was up to the European immigrants who arrived in the 1846 to finally establish the town.

San Marcos has an interesting town center and has two areas that are **National Register Historic Places:** the downtown district, and the San Antonio and Belvin Streets residential districts. There is a two-mile long scenic walkway along the river that starts just two blocks from the courthouse on the town square. It is famous locally for the huge outlet malls on the outskirts of town along I-35.

After 10 miles Hwy. 12 goes to the right; take this turn and continue on Hwy. 12 for five more miles. Take a right turn onto Hwy. 3237 in Wimberley. If you are hungry, **Wimberley** has several places for a meal or snack. Just past the intersection of Hwys. 12 and 3237, there's a good barbeque place on the right that offers outdoor dining.

Soon, you will be leaving the built-up area around New Braunsfels and San Marcos to get back to some wonderful Hill Country riding. After 12 miles, turn left onto Hwy. 150 west in Hays City (one general store); this is an easy turn to miss, so be on the lookout. After 11 delightful miles of riding, take a right turn onto Hwy. 12; two miles later, go left onto Hwy. 290 in Dripping Springs. Go less than a mile down Hwy. 290 and take a left onto Hwy. 190 (Creek Road). The sign is very small, but there is a larger sign indicating Loop 64 opposite it.

Creek Road becomes a one-lane, two-way road—one of many that exist in the Hill Country. It also has several one-lane bridges along its nine-mile path. This is just another (ho-hum) super bike ride. Three miles after the turn-off from Hwy. 290, Creek Road intersects with County Road 220 and makes a right turn (don't go straight on County Road 220). At the intersection with Hwy. 165, take a left.

Hwy. 165 runs alongside the **Blanco River.** After 15 miles, at the T-intersection with Loop 163, take a right into Blanco. When Loop 163 intersects with Hwy. 281, go straight across, to get on Hwy. 1623. After five miles, turn left onto Hwy. 1888. The 28 miles to the intersection with Hwy. 1376

Wildflowers

The roadsides and pasturelands of Texas are blanketed with blue, yellow, rust, and red wildflowers. Spring months in the hill country are worthy of a special note. Colorful autumn leaves lure others from different parts of the country. Monet would go wild! Just south of Austin, the National Wildflower Research Center (512-292-4200), founded by Lady Bird Johnson in 1982, contains interactive exhibits and examples of all the native flora of Texas. To plan your trip for "peak" viewing, contact the state tourism bureau at 800-452-9292. As a rider, realize that at any time, you could round a turn on a small rural road only to find it all but blocked with cars and photographers.   ✪

If you ride the hill country in the spring, mile after mile of beautiful wildflowers will greet you.

are just great, high-speed, Hill Country roads.

Turn right onto Hwy. 1376. If you haven't yet visited **Luckenbach,** go two miles up Hwy. 1376 and turn left just across the bridge. After seven miles on Hwy. 1376, turn left onto Hwy. 290. Five miles later, you will be in Fredericksburg.

Loop 5 Y.O. Ranch

Distance *215 miles*
Features *This loop consists mostly of high-speed roads that are somewhat straighter than usual for the Hill Country. However, you will find many curves, sweepers, and twisties along the way. While it is set up as a one-day trip, I recommend you make it a two-day ride with an overnight stop at the Y.O. Ranch. In spite of the deserted countryside, there are plenty of small towns and a state park with good wildlife viewing to visit along the way.*

From the intersection of Hwys. 290/87 and 16 in Fredericksburg, take Hwy. 16 south for approximately four miles and then make a right turn onto Hwy. 2093. The 22 miles that follow are a lot flatter and straighter than most Hill Country roads, but you are treated to an almost constant view of the beautiful terrain through which you are riding.

Turn left onto Hwy. 290 in Harper, go four miles, and then turn right onto Hwy. 479. The constant up and down and up and down on this road

The exotic animals are very friendly at the Y.O. Ranch.

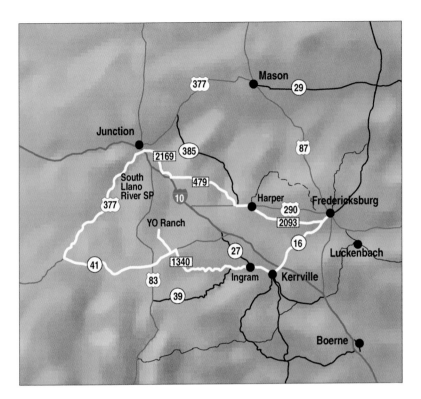

will remind you of a roller coaster thickly lined with cedar trees. In the Hill Country, cedar trees are considered a nuisance, as they tend to choke out the live oak trees. It is unusual to see such an abundant growth, as most landowners clear them out.

After about 20 miles, at a T-intersection, turn right onto Hwy. 2169, toward the town of Junction. Four miles later, as you are approaching the intersection with I-10, turn right just before the STOP sign to continue on Hwy. 2169. Along this stretch, notice the many pecan groves with huge trees. The pecans that have been developing here since 1896 are known throughout the world. The **Oliver pecan**, named after the man who developed them, can produce up to 350 to 400 pounds of nuts per year.

After approximately 9 miles you will be approaching I-10. Take the overpass across the interstate, proceed one mile, then turn right onto Loop 481. You will enter the town of Junction upon crossing the river.

About one mile after turning onto Loop 481, take a left onto Hwy. 377. Prepare for 43 miles of magnificent motorcycling. Four miles along this wonderful road, you will find the **South Llano River State Park**, an excellent public park with camping facilities, hiking trails, river tubing, and

Texans love exotic animal ranches. You never know what you'll see around the next bend. (photo by Jack Lewis/TxDOT)

many other activities. The deer, wild turkeys, and wildlife for which the park is known are somewhat accustomed to people and can be viewed at very close range. If you are a camper, an overnight stay here would be a true joy. If you just want to ride through and see the wildlife, let them know at the entrance and the $3 entrance fee will be waived for your short visit.

While Hwy. 377 is a major thruway, it is considered by many to be the most scenic road in the Hill Country. From the motorcyclist's viewpoint, it is not only scenic, but also a great ride. While you can make good time on this road, it does have a few surprises; I suggest you keep your speed down; many of the curves along this ride have a suggested 30 mph speed limit. Enjoy the high limestone cliffs along the **South Llano River** covered with trees and other vegetation.

After 43 miles of fun on Hwy. 377, turn left onto Hwy. 41, which is more high-speed than Hwy. 377. After about 33 miles, the entrance to the Y.O. Ranch will be on your left. Once consisting of more than 500,000 acres, the **Y.O. Ranch** is now only a measly (by Texas standards) 40,000 acres. But to put that in perspective: it is more than seven miles from the entrance gate to the lodge. I highly recommend a visit.

A handy café, the **Chuckwagon,** serves three meals a day that are included in the price of your room.

More than 10,000 animals roam freely over the Y.O. Ranch, of which about 60 percent are exotics from all over the world (mostly Africa). A hunter can choose his prey from upwards of forty species, which include addax ($5,000), dama gazelle ($4,500) or, for those of you on a budget, wild turkey (only $450). Of course, these fees do not include the $200 fee and a tip for your guide, who can also provide you with a rifle and other equipment. Some of the native animals can be shot without charge. Hone your skills before embarking, as a wounded animal costs just as much as a kill here.

Many people come to the Y.O. Ranch to hunt with only a camera. A two-hour tour ($30 including a meal) is available several times a day. The giraffe will eat corn from your hand. Bring plenty of film and enjoy your safari! A one-day advance reservation is required for tours and lodging.

Although exotic animals are the big draw, the Y.O. remains a working cattle ranch, and the friendly staff can help you schedule some horseback

At the Y.O. Ranch, a hunter with about $5,000 handy could take aim at this fellow. Many folks come to take a tour and merely photo-hunt.

Pecan orchards are throughout the hill country. This local variety, the Oliver, named after its founder, will yield up to 400 pounds of pecans each year and is now grown worldwide.

riding. If you time it right, you could even go on an overnight cattle drive (a la *City Slickers).*

I highly recommend an overnight at the ranch. Camping is available as are cabins (*Sandy's Choice*—$150), and motel rooms. A handy café, the **Chuckwagon**, is located near the lodging area and serves three meals a day that are included in your room charge. Also a free open bar is available in the evening for several hours. There is a very nice swimming pool and hot tub near the lodging area. RV camping costs $20 per night with meals priced at about $10 each.

In spite of the size of this place, there are limited camping and motel accommodations, so plan your visit for during the week and give as much advance notice as possible (800-967-2624; www.yoranch.com).

After your visit to the ranch, return to the main road, continue east on Hwy. 41 for another two miles, and then turn right onto Hwy. 1340, a road for which Hill Country riding is famous. It has something for everyone: sport bikers can test themselves and their machines and cruisers can enjoy the wonderful scenery.

Around every curve in the Hill Country, limestone cliffs and flowing rivers await you.

After about 19 miles, you will encounter another of those almost endless oddities that cover Texas and reflect the eclectic natures of its residents. On the right side of the road, sitting in a pasture, is a **full-size model of Stonehenge,** in better repair than the original in England. You are welcomed to visit the site at no charge.

Twenty-one miles after turning on Hwy. 1340, turn left onto Hwy. 39 toward Ingram. Rolling along the **Guadalupe River,** this road begs to be enjoyed. While fairly well developed, there is usually little or no traffic along it during the week. After only six miles, you will come to the intersection with Hwy. 27, where the road becomes four-lane as it approaches Kerrville (see the Guadaloupe Fork Road description for more about Kerrville). Seven miles after passing through Kerrville, turn left onto Hwy. 16. Fredericksburg is only 25 miles up the road.

Day 7   Fredericksburg to San Antonio

Distance *90 miles*
Features *Visit a wildflower farm—an opportunity you don't want to miss in the spring; take a short side trip to the LBJ Ranch complex if you didn't have the time on that loop. You'll end up near the San Antonio airport.*

From downtown Fredericksburg, proceed east on Hwy. 290. About eight miles later, start looking for the wildflower ranch on your left—a clearly marked, multi-story building sitting out in the middle of a field. In the spring and summer, with the wildflowers blooming, it is an incredible feast for the eyes.

After 16 miles on this good, high speed, four-lane road, turn right onto Hwy. 1623. The **LBJ Ranch** complex is only two miles further down Hwy. 290 from this turn, should you wish to visit (see the Fredericksburg to Austin Loop for details).

Hwy. 1623 twists and turns, and goes up and down, often running alongside the **Blanco River**. After 16 miles of this fun, turn right onto County Road 103, which has a posted speed limit of 30 mph and often 20 mph. It has a few river crossings that could be wet after a rainy spell, as well as some open range sections. Slow down and enjoy!

Many area motorcyclists meet in Luckenbach on Sunday afternoons to swap lies, kick tires, and drink Lone Star beer.

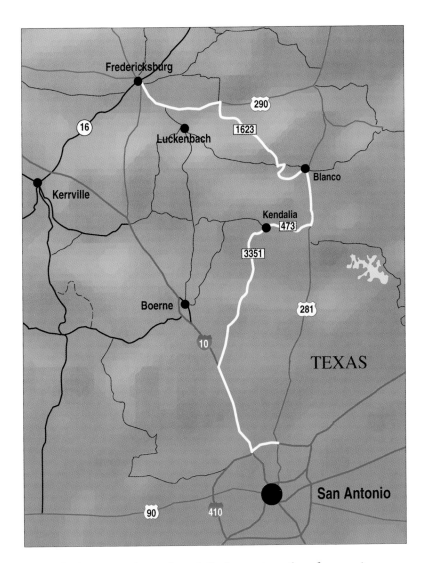

At the T-intersection, take a left. Some six miles after turning onto Trainer West, take the right turn at the T-intersection onto Ficher Street. You will be in Blanco, a few short blocks from where you will turn right onto Hwy. 281. Eight miles later, turn right onto Hwy. 473. After eight miles on Hwy. 473, make a left turn onto Hwy. 3351 in Kendalia.

Savor the remaining 23 miles to I-10, before you start to see more development, with huge ranch houses sitting atop the hills alongside the road. Take I-10 east and 13 miles later you will be at the intersection with Loop 410. To get to the airport area, take Loop 410 east.

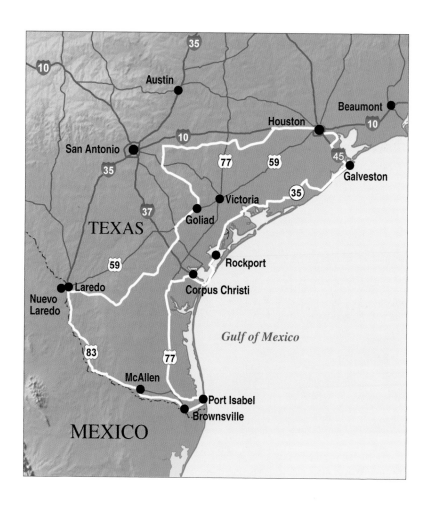

The Coastal Route

Starting and ending in Houston, this route consists of six days of riding and covers more than 1,200 miles of seacoast and marshland, brushy scrublands with rolling hills, and live oak forests, skirting the southern boundary of the Hill Country. This area also showcases the diverse people who call themselves Texans; from the sophisticated of metropolitan Houston to the laid-back fishermen and pleasure seekers that dominate the coastal regions.

You will travel through the fertile Rio Grande Valley along the route known as *Los Caminos Del Rio* (the roads of the river), to the vast openness of South Central Texas with its rolling hills covered with mesquite and cactus and towns bordering Mexico where the large Hispanic population gives you a flavor of life in that nation.

Starting and ending in the city of Houston, the final day will find you at two of the most important sites in Texas history now populated by the descendents of European settlers that have retained much of the "old world" flavor. You can visit the world's largest cattle ranch or day-trip into Mexico

Skyscrapers sprout like mushrooms from the flat lands on which Houston is located.
(photo by Jack Lewis/TxDOT)

or connect with one of our over the border trips. I suggest that you plan on a minimum of seven days to truly experience this trip with its diversity, open roads, and motorcycle touring at its best.

Approaching a population of three and a half million, **Houston** is the third largest city in the United States. It is a sprawling metropolis containing almost 600 square miles within its city limits. Skyscrapers leap from the flat landscape like weeds in a well-groomed lawn—works of structural art in their own right. At night, these clusters of giants glow with light, creating a truly awesome sight. Not limited to the downtown area, skyscrapers are found in clusters all over. The 64-story Transco tower is located more than six miles from downtown. The terrain is flat and low with the highest elevation in the city limits reaching only ninety feet above sea level. Houston is the largest international seaport in the country, although it is more than fifty miles from the Gulf of Mexico. As you would expect from a city this size, Houston has more than 200 museums, cultural sites, and other places to visit. Houstonians are very proud of their arts. Their symphony, ballet, and theater are comparable to any in the world.

While exploring the many wildlife refuges along the south Texas coast and the bayous of east Texas, be aware the waters may not always be friendly. (photo by Jack Lewis/TxDOT)

Houston was founded by **John** and **Augustus Allen** in 1836, when they established a trading post on **Buffalo Bayou**. The climate was truly brutal with heat, high humidity, and hordes of insects. From the beginning, Houston established a reputation for being a rough-and-tumble, high-stakes city, and it works hard to maintain that reputation to this day. The Houston attitude is exemplified in the city's zoning laws: they have none.

Houston's location and climate kept its development moving at a slow pace until the 1930s; the miracle of air conditioning, however, changed all that. Today, most Houstonians move from their air-conditioned homes to their air-conditioned cars to their air-conditioned workplaces, rarely encountering the sweltering heat. Some of the parking lots in Houston are even air conditioned. A new visitor often notes that there is almost no pedestrian traffic downtown, even during a lunch hour on a working day. In fact, there is a huge underground tunnel system (air-conditioned, of course) that connects most of the downtown buildings, and contains shops, restaurants, and everything else one should need in daily life.

With the discovery of massive amounts of oil at **Spindletop** in 1901, Houston quickly became the new hub for the oil business. Today it is estimated that 35 percent of its economy is based on oil and oil related businesses. All major companies and hundreds of independents are represented, and some of them claim Houston as their home. The influx of money they bring to the city is a boon for local entrepreneurs who are interested in serving their needs. As a result, the shopping opportunities are limitless.

Although the oil industry brings in the money, the **Texas Medical Center** is the largest employer in Houston. Consisting of more than 40 institutions covering almost 700 acres near downtown, they offer state-of-the-art medical services to a worldwide clientele. For more information on things to see and do in Houston check out their visitors' center website at www.houston-guide.com.

Houston has two major airports, **George Bush Intercontinental**, located 20 miles north of downtown, and **William P. Hobby** about 10 miles southwest of downtown. If you are flying in, try to use the smaller and closer Hobby. Obviously with any city this size, lodgings in every price range and category are plentiful. One special place of note, *(Sandy's Choice)*, is the Four Seasons, 1300 Lamar Street (713-652-6220, www.fourseasons.com). Food options are endless and many are world class.

Day 1   Houston to Galveston

Distance *83 miles; 143 miles with the side trip*
Features *This short ride will get you out of the city. The rest of your day should be spent sightseeing at some of the many sites worthy of your attention, including the San Jacinto Monument, located on the battleground where Texas won her independence from Mexico; the Lyndon B. Johnson Space Center (NASA headquarters); and the famous Galveston historic district. If you want to ride more, take an 80-mile run along the scenic oceanfront out to the end of Galveston Island and back.*

The San Jacinto Monument marks the location of the battle where Texas won her independence from Mexico.

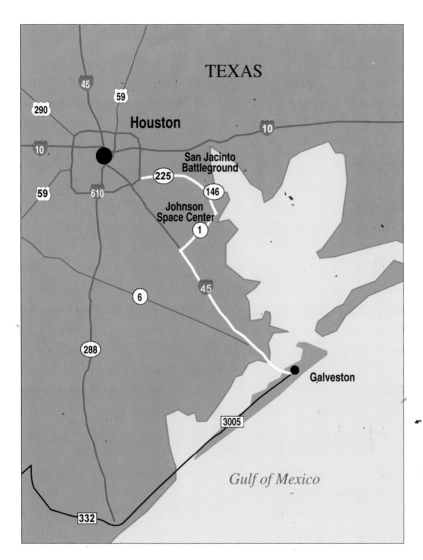

The freeway system in and around Houston is not for the faint of heart. The
traffic is heavy and the drivers are aggressive. Hang in there and stay alert as
you navigate your way out of town. Starting at the intersection of I-45 and
Loop 610 south of town, take Loop 610 east. After only two miles, take Exit
30B onto Hwy. 225 (La Porte Freeway) toward Pasadena. You will soon go
through the towns of Deer Park and Pasadena. Most people are overwhelmed the first time through here by the sights and smells of the massive
crude oil refineries and petrochemical plants that line this road. This area is
the bedrock on which the Houston economy rests.

After 11 miles, exit onto Battleground Road (Hwy. 134) and follow signs to the **San Jacinto Monument.** Just 2-1/2 miles up this road, take a right to the battleground and monument.

Warning: If you choose not to make the pilgrimage to San Jacinto, you would be wise not to admit this to any Texan, lest you risk bodily injury or at least a good tongue-lashing.

The **San Jacinto Historical Complex** is located on the site where the Texicans defeated **General Santa Anna** and his army on April 21, 1836, to secure their independence from Mexico. It was not much of a battle by today's standards: fewer than 1,000 Mexican soldiers were killed and only 9 Texicans.

Attacking during the traditional *siesta* time, the Texicans were able to obtain complete surprise. The Mexicans reportedly attempted to surrender only 18 minutes into the battle, but the Texicans continued the killing for almost two hours shouting, "Remember the Alamo!" and "Remember Goliad!" Rumor has it that when the battle commenced, Santa Anna was being distracted by a mulatto slave woman who'd been sneaked into the

Wildlife refuges along the Texas gulf coast are famous for their birds.
(photo by Randy Green/TxDOT)

Mexican camp. It's hard to lead troops with your pants down. The song, *The Yellow Rose of Texas* commemorates her contribution to Texan independence.

The battleground is marked by a 570-foot limestone obelisk said to be tallest in the world, 15 feet taller than the Washington Monument. An elevator can take you to an observation deck from which you can get a good view of what remains lovingly preserved of the original battleground—surrounded by Houston's industrial complexes, downtown bustle, and ship channel. A museum outlines early Texas history and shows a short film, *Texas Forever!* narrated by **Charlton Heston**, which expounds upon the events that took place here.

Leaving the battleground, follow the signs directing you to the permanent mooring of **the battleship Texas,** the last surviving battleship to serve in both World War I and World War II. It has been extensively renovated and is open for tours. From the battleship you can get a close look at the huge tankers carrying crude oil, petroleum products, and petrochemicals in and out of the ship channel.

After your visit to the San Jacinto Complex, retrace your route on Hwy. 134 to the intersection with Hwy. 225 and turn left. After four miles, turn right (south) onto 146. From this point, you will still be in an urban area, but the traffic thins to some extent and you can give your nerves a rest. After nine miles take a right onto NASA Road 1 in Clear Lake. If you go over the huge bridge into Kemah, you will have gone too far. **Clear Lake** offers a wonderful sheltered cove for yachts and boats of every description, with access to the Gulf of Mexico via **Galveston Bay.**

Six miles along NASA Road 1, you'll see the **Lyndon B. Johnson Space Center** on your right, mission control for all NASA space operations. To see the facility, you must first visit **Space Center Houston,** located on your right about a block past the NASA entranceway. Several interesting exhibits and films outline the U.S. space program, and some of the original spacecraft are on display, including the last one to land on the moon. You can even touch a real moon rock. Trams to the NASA facility itself operate on an almost continuous basis. You can visit mission control, check out the astronaut training complex, and examine a training mock-up of a space shuttle. Many people spend a whole day here.

The quickest and easiest way to reach your destination of **Galveston Island** is to continue on NASA 1 until the intersection with I-45. From there, you head south for approximately 28 miles until you cross the bridge onto the island. As you travel along this road, the traffic thins, and you will soon be in a rural area of vast marshlands. After crossing onto the island, the road becomes Broadway (Avenue J). Continue straight ahead until you reach the ocean.

Galveston does not put its best foot forward as you enter the city. You will pass through some fairly seedy neighborhoods. However, as you approach the ocean, the restored Victorian homes begin to brighten your view. When you can see the ocean, turn right, to put yourself on Seawall Blvd. (for some reason, this intersection is marked as 6th Street).

Side Trip

If you have the time, you can continue on this road to the end of the island, about 40 miles away. The ride out and back is very straightforward and scenic, with lots of places to take in the ocean beaches and bayside marshes.

The city and island of **Galveston** have had a "boom and bust" history. Not much is known about its early inhabitants, as periodic hurricanes have destroyed any remains or artifacts. When the area was discovered by white men, the **Karankawa Indians** were living here, but it didn't take long before they were driven from their homeland to west Texas, where they died out. Both the Spanish and French made unsuccessful attempts to found permanent settlements. In 1817, the buccaneer **Jean Lafitte** established the pirate stronghold of **Campeachy,** but it lasted only four short years, though they were no doubt rough and rowdy times. Legends of buried treasure persist to this day.

During the Civil War, Galveston was captured by Union forces and then recaptured by the Confederates. After the war, Galveston became the most modern city in Texas and prospered as the nation's third-largest port and a major banking center. But everything changed on September 8, 1900, when a massive hurricane completely destroyed Galveston and killed an estimated 6,000 of its 36,000 residents. The ten-mile seawall we see today was built for protection, and the elevation of the city was raised almost 20 feet behind this seawall. Despite these measures, Galveston never recovered from this event, and shipping and business interests moved inland to Houston.

In the 1930s and '40s an attempt was made to revive the island's economy by making it into a gambling haven. Massive efforts by law enforcement shut down this illegal activity in the 1950s, as the city had become dangerous. By the 1960s, Galveston had carved a promising niche for itself as a port that primarily handled fruits and produce. Today, this is the base of the economy, with tourism a strong second. Another attraction to

Expect breath-taking views of the gulf waters as you ride along the Texas coast.

Galveston, other than its beaches and oceanfront, is the more than 1,500 restored **Victorian homes**, 500 of which are on the National Historic Register.

There is a good selection of motels and hotels in Galveston in every price range. A good medium-priced place to stay is **Gaido's Seaside Inn** located at 3802 Seawall Blvd. (www.gaidosofgalveston.com, 409-762-9626, 800-525-0064, $90). As anywhere else, a room with an ocean view commands a premium; you can save about $20 if you don't mind a view of a parking lot. Note also that the fenced, locked parking area for these rooms is quieter and more secure than the one facing Seawall.

Gaido's restaurant, next to the inn, is deemed by many to be the best place to eat on the island. Run by the same family for more than 85 years, they serve up huge portions of great seafood. Nevertheless, this place can be pricey and you might not be comfortable in your casual clothes. **Casey's Seafood Restaurant,** located in the motel, has the same fare at a much lower price, as it has the same owners and operators as Gaido's.

If budget is no problem, stay at the **Tremont House** *(Sandy's Choice)* at 2300 Mechanic Street (409-763-0300, $160 and up), an 1800s building that was converted to a luxury hotel in the 1980s with no expense spared. It contains a nice courtyard and rooftop bar from which you can enjoy the sunset.

The nearest camping to the city of Galveston is about six miles southwest off Seawall Blvd., on 61st S.E. at **Galveston Island State Park** (409-737-1222, $20). This is a beautiful setting with nature trails that go from the ocean on one side to the bay on the other. The oceanside camping is usually more crowded; the bay side is more remote on a beautiful marsh but can get pretty hot and buggy on a still night. If you wish, there are a limited number of screened shelters available for a few dollars more per night. If you are really lucky you will be there when a Broadway musical is being preformed in its outdoor theater. Galveston State Park accepts reservations and the facilities include flush toilets, showers, grills, and picnic tables. Turn left at the sign to get your space assigned and pay before settling in.

The **Galveston Convention and Visitors Bureau** (www.galveston.com) at 2106 Seawall offers an amazing array of brochures on things to do and see on the island. If you are interested in seeing the many Victorian homes in comfort, a trolley will take you through the **Strand** and the **Silk Stocking,**

This "jack-up" drilling rig is ready to find some more of that "Texas Tea."

The Bishop's Palace in Galveston is just on of the many fine, old Victorian homes that have been restored in this city by the sea.

two of the historic districts. The cost is only $1 and you can park your bike at the center.

To get an idea of how the rich of Galveston lived during its heyday, visit **The Grand,** the opera house built in 1894. Located at 2020 Post Office, it is a magnificent building. Self-guided tours are available of the interior. **Sarah Bernhardt, Paderewski, Anna Pavlova, John Philip Sousa, Helen Hayes,** and the **Vienna Boys Choir** are among those who have performed here. It is true opulence.

The **Bishop's Palace,** located at 1402 Broadway, will be on your left as you enter Galveston. The **American Institute of Architecture** has designated this Victorian structure as the second most impressive in the United States. It was built in 1886 at an estimated cost of $250,000 by **Colonel Walter Gresham.** In 1923, it was purchased by the Galveston-Houston Diocese as a home for the late **Bishop Christopher Byrne,** thereby gaining the name of Bishop's Palace. After the bishop's death in 1950 it was opened to the public. Original in every detail and carefully preserved, tours are offered daily. If you plan to see only one of these homes, this one is the one to see.

Day 2 Galveston to Rockport

Distance *210 miles*
Features *Miles of riding along the south Texas coast, an opportunity to ride your bike on the beach, views of massive petrochemical plants, and a visit to one of the largest and most interesting wildlife preserves in the world will make this an interesting and full day.*

From your hotel in Galveston, ride west on Seawall Blvd. You will soon leave the built-up zone of city services and find yourself passing by numerous beach homes built atop stilts. The area then quickly turns to open sand dunes and marshland. After roughly six miles, **Galveston Island State Park** straddles the entire island. The park headquarters on the left is a good place to get off the bike and take a stroll on the beach to enjoy the fresh sea breezes. If you turn right here, there is a nice, short loop through the marshes to the bay with campers and RVs dotted about.

About 30 miles from downtown Galveston, you come to the end of the island and cross over the **San Luis Pass Bridge** (toll) onto **Follets Island**. From there, the next 13 miles to the resort town of **Surfside Beach** is a

Sights such as these bring birders from around the world to south Texas. (photo by TxDOT)

beautiful ride along the ocean. At several points, you can access the beach with your motorcycle and once there, you can amble along with the sea lapping at your wheels. Most of the access points consist of good hardpack, but you should probably avoid the ones where you can see loose sand between the pavement and the hard-packed beach. The beach surface between the high and low tide marks is good and many motorcyclists and automobiles travel it everyday. Should you wish to stop and enjoy for a while, be sure to have a foot handy for your side stand and keep an eye on the tide. This place is almost deserted during the week and has very few people on it even on the weekends.

At the traffic light in Surfside Beach you should take a right onto Hwy. 332. Keep your eye out as you approach this light as there are usually giant offshore drilling rigs, known as "jack-up" rigs in this area. You can ride up to them and see just how big and complicated these monsters are.

After crossing over the bridge to the mainland, you will enter the town of **Freeport**, a heavily industrialized area thick with petrochemical plants. At the first traffic light, turn left onto Hwy. 523 (a sign also points to Hwy. 36). Continue to work your way through this developed area following signs to Hwy. 36. After about seven miles, Hwy. 36 takes off to the right at the yellow flashing light. It is obvious that Hwy. 36 was built by dredging the marshes. As a result, it has nice stretches of water along both sides. Many people will be fishing or casting nets in an attempt to catch the bounty contained therein.

Soon you will cross the **Intracoastal Waterway** and gradually gain a small amount of altitude. As you do this, the marshland gives way to live oak woods and an occasional farm. After about 16 miles, turn left onto Hwy. 521. The next 28 miles make for a very pleasant ride through lush vegetation with many stream crossings and pecan groves. While this road is primarily straight, there are quite a few S-curves scattered along to keep your attention.

At the T-intersection in Wadsworth turn left as Hwy. 521 joins Hwy. 60, then after a very short distance, turn right to stay with Hwy. 521 as it leaves Hwy. 60. The landscape for the next 21 miles will consist of huge farms reaching as far as the eye can see. The most dramatic feature along this ride is a nuclear power plant with high-voltage power lines stretching to the horizon. A nice roadside stop explains its history and operation.

Turn left onto Hwy. 35 and continue five miles to the small town of **Palacios** (pop. 4,500). This small town lives on because an enormous fishing fleet calls this home. Seafood processing plants here get the catch ready for market. To get a good look at the fleet as you come into town, take Hwy. 35 Business and then turn left at the sign indicating the public boat ramp. At the end of the street that runs along the bay, retrace your route and make a left onto Hwy. 35 Business to continue on your way. Hwy. 35 Business shortly rejoins Hwy. 35 where you should turn left (south). The next few miles offer attractive views of the many bays along which the road runs.

After approximately 26 miles you will cross over a long bridge and enter the town of **Port Lavaca**. As one would assume while traveling along a stretch of road bordering on the gulf, you can get good, fresh seafood in every town. Just after leaving the bridge in Port Lavaca, however, there's a place on your right that is unusual for the area. **Gordon's Seafood Grill** doesn't look like much from the road, but the interior is very upscale and the seafood is prepared in an epicurean fashion. If you desire something other than the usual fried or boiled fish, shrimp, or crab, try this place. Be forewarned—it is somewhat pricey.

Continue on Hwy. 35 south for about 23 miles and make a left turn onto Hwy. 239 in Maudlowe. The first few miles of this run pass through farmland and then becomes marshier. There are many wildlife preserves through here which resemble the Florida Everglades.

The turns to the **Aransas Pass Wildlife Refuge** are well-marked: after about four miles, Hwy. 239 ends in the small town of Austwell. Make a

Shrimping is a major industry along the Gulf Coast of Texas. The fleet works at night and rests during the day. It doesn't get any fresher than this! (photo by Jack Lewis/TxDOT)

right turn onto Hwy. 774. Continue for one mile and then turn left onto Hwy. 2040. After seven miles of riding on this increasingly narrow road, with the terrain growing swampy, you will find yourself at the refuge head-quarters (www.fws.gov/southwest/refuges/texas/aransas). Aransas is the winter home of the **whooping crane**, which is making a slow comeback from near extinction. The estimated worldwide population of these birds in 1945 was 15; the present count numbers more than 400.

After visiting the reception building that has several exhibits outlining the various types of animals that inhabit the refuge, you can ride five miles into the park to an observation tower to look out over part of the parks 115,000 acres.

If you wish, you may return to the entrance via an eleven-mile one-way paved road through the backlands, which gives you an opportunity to see close-up the varying landscapes that make up this wonderful place. Various roadside exhibits explain what you are seeing. Please honor the 15 and 25 mph speed limits as the park is inhabited by deer, javelinas, bobcats, rac-coons, alligators, turtles, frogs, snakes, and hundreds of bird species. The deer have become especially accustomed to the traffic and you may find the

The whooping crane population is making a nice comeback wintering in the Aransas Park Wildlife Refuge and co-existing with the oil industry nearby. (photo by TxDOT)

road around any curve completely blocked. If you plan to take any of the many hiking trails or spend a good deal of time off your bike, pick up some bug repellant at headquarters.

Leaving the refuge, retrace your route to the intersection with Hwy. 774 and make a left turn. While this road proceeds mostly flat and straight through farmland, it does have a few unmarked 90-degree turns along its nine miles. Stay alert. Turn left onto Hwy. 35 south at the intersection and proceed approximately 13 miles to the left turn on Park Road 13 into **Goose Island State Park.** At the STOP sign, go straight ahead. This small road meanders around and then goes to the left along the seaside.

As the road turns left away from the ocean, the **Big Tree,** also known as the Lamar Oak or the Bishop Oak, will be on your right. The largest oak tree in Texas, it has a circumference of 35 feet, stands 44 feet tall, and has a crown of 89 feet. It is estimated to be more than 1,000 years old, and sitting as it does right on the gulf, one can only wonder how many hurricanes it has survived.

After your visit, continue on the small road through the oak groves, turning left at the T-intersection, and right at the four-way stop. Then retrace your route to Hwy. 35 where you should turn left. This little loop down to see the tree is only two or three miles and will not take much time.

If you are camping, sites are available in the   **Goose Island State Park** itself, with almost all the services you will need for a wonderful night nestled in a live oak forest. There is no food here, however. If you prefer to be in a more urban setting, continue on to Rockport to the **Ancient Oaks RV Park** located at 1222 Hwy. 35 south; their facilities include a laundry room, fishing pier, and swimming pool.

Hwy. 35 takes you over the long bridge spanning **Copano Bay.** Another three miles will bring you to a left turn onto Fulton Beach Road. You will soon be running along the seafront with modern condominiums sharing the area with several old mansions.

A more than adequate "mom and pop" place to stay is the **Bayfront Cottages** (www.rockportbayfrontcottages.com, 361-729-6693, $65) located next to the Fulton Mansion. Should you prefer more modern accommodations, continue to the intersection with Hwy. 35 and turn left into Rockport proper where you will find all the national chains represented. There are plenty of good places to eat, but for a unique treat, try the **Boiling Pot** located on Fulton Beach Road at Palmetto Street. Shrimp, crab, and raw fish are boiled in water rich with Cajun spices and then deposited directly onto your paper-covered table for your further handling. For an extra treat, try a cup of the gumbo.

The cities of **Rockport** and **Fulton,** separated in name only, abut each other with no noticeable boundaries. With a combined population of approximately 7,000, the mainstay of the local economy is fishing. Originally developed by the **Morgan Steamship Company** as a port for shipping Texas beef to the northeast, the advent of the railroad put it into a quick decline. The old mansions along the coast are the only reminders of the glory days. The **Fulton Mansion State Historical Structure,** located on Fulton Beach Road just after entering the Rockport city limits, is a most magnificent example. Built in the 1870s by a cattle baron, it has been restored in all its grandeur. Guided tours are available to show you around and explain the history and uniqueness of this home.

These days, Rockport considers itself the premier artists' colony in Texas and many galleries showcase the local wares. Tourism is also becoming more and more important, and all the usual beach activities are well represented. If you want to see more of the **Aransas Wildlife Refuge,** several boat tours leave regularly from the beachfront.

Day 3 Rockport to Port Isabel

Distance *220 miles*

Features *This day offers yet more chances to explore beautiful south Texas beaches, visit some small fishing villages, and travel through the vast farmlands that make this the breadbasket of Texas and much of the nation. You can check out the world's largest ranch and the town that grew from it. The day ends either in a picturesque fishing village, or a modern world-class beach resort town, as you wish.*

A visit to the Fulton Mansion in Rockport will give you an idea how the "rich and famous" cattle barons lived in an earlier era. (photo by Bill Reaves/TxDOT)

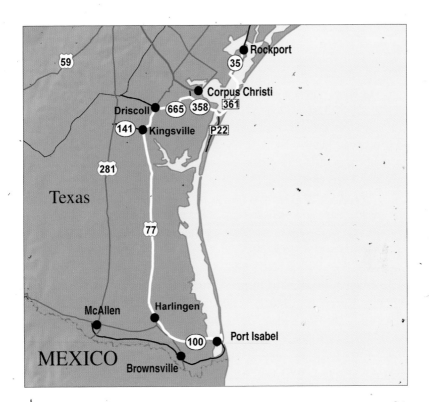

From downtown Rockport, continue south on Hwy. 35 for approximately eight miles and make a left onto Loop 90 to Port Aransas and to Hwy. 361. When you come to the intersection with Hwy. 361, take a left and proceed seven more miles to the ferry crossing onto Mustang Island. The five-minute ferry ride is free and operates 24 hours a day. After departing the ferry, you should take the first right and continue on Hwy. 361 for approximately 18 miles to the intersection with Park Road 22 on the outskirts of Corpus Christi.

Virtually undeveloped except for the small town of **Port Aransas** in the north, **Mustang Island** has some of the best beaches in Texas. Historically, the fishing village was very difficult to get to, and this suited the locals just fine. With the extension of Hwy. 361 a few years back, this place became much more accessible and a few condos appeared at the south end of town, but it hasn't yet lost its laid-back beach lifestyle.

Hwy. 361 down the center of Mustang Island splits through the rolling sand dunes covered with sea oats. You can ride your motorcycle on the beach, but yesterday's caveats still apply.

Side Trip

At the intersection with Park Road 22 you can take a left and run about five miles on a paved road to the **Padre Island National Seashore Visitors' Center,** which contains interesting exhibits regarding the world's longest coastal barrier island (113 miles). The pavement extends only about a mile past the center, but you can then continue on the beach if you want. Be aware, however, that the riding surface soon deteriorates and becomes impassable after about five miles.

After your visit to Padre Island, return out of the park on Park Road 22 and connect with Hwy. 358 into Corpus Christi (straight ahead). This highway soon becomes four-lane and then a major freeway traversing this city.

Corpus Christi is a thriving town with a population estimated at close to 400,000. It grew up as a raunchy port city, first known for its smuggling activities, and later for its bars, strip clubs, and the associated businesses that served the sailors and naval pilots based here. It has outgrown this image and is now a major port and home base for vast oil refining and processing industry. Corpus Christi is not known as a tourist destination, but rather as a jumping off point to the areas around it (see www.cctexas.com for sights). The most popular attraction here is retired carrier, the **USS Lexington,** located on the ship channel at 2914 N. Shoreline Blvd. This carrier served in WWII and was on active duty until 1962 when it became a training ship. When it was retired from service in 1991, the city purchased it and moved it here. Several exhibits outline its history and capabilities. If you have never been on one of these ships, you will be astonished by its size.

Approximately 18 miles after getting on Hwy. 358, exit the freeway and turn left onto Hwy. 665 (Old Brownsville Road). Once you get onto Hwy. 665, you quickly leave the city behind for farmland. For the next 21 miles this road is flat and straight, though you have to make a clearly marked right turn at one point to continue on it. A few stiff curves occur here and there, but they are all marked with yellow flashing lights. When you intersect with Hwy. 77 in the town of Driscoll, turn left. After approximately 13 miles of straight, high-speed road, take a right onto King Street (Hwy. 141) in Kingsville.

Kingsville, the only town in the county of Kleberg, is the home of the world famous King Ranch (www.king-ranch.com). Founded by Rio Grande riverboat captain **Richard King** in 1853, the ranch now has

Lush vegetation, beaches, and commercial activities such as fishing and the oil industry enjoy a peaceful co-existence along the Texas gulf coast. (photo Tx/DOT.).

holdings in Texas exceeding 1.2 million acres (the base ranch here, 825,000 acres, is larger than the state of Rhode Island). Currently owned by more than 100 of Captain King's heirs, the **King Ranch** operates as a multi-national corporation with worldwide holdings exceeding four million acres. The first American breed of beef cattle, the Santa Gertrudis, was established on the King Ranch, and its horse breeding has produced several Derby winners.

A visitor's center to the ranch, located approximately two miles straight ahead on highway 141 on your left, offers 90-minute air-conditioned bus tours of parts of the ranch. You will see cowboys on horses working much the same as they did in the past, along with grazing cattle, miles of fences, and original ranch homes and buildings. The visitor's center also houses a few exhibits of the early days of the ranch. A much more complete collection of photographs and memorabilia, as well as a video presentation on the ranch's history, is located at 405 N 6th St. To get there from the ranch headquarters just go straight across highway 141 onto Santa Gertrudis to 6th Street and turn right.

As luck would have it, the King Ranch also was sitting on a pool of oil,

Unless you're looking for a job, be sure and take a left as you approach the entrance to the King Ranch.

and this industry has become yet another important part of the Kingsville economy. Today, with a population of almost 30,000, Kingsville has a branch of **Texas A&M University** and a naval air station. If you are hungry, try **Los Amigos Restaurant** at 1920 E. King. It has a daily all-you-can-eat buffet featuring some of the finest Tex-Mex food you will ever encounter.

From the intersection of Hwys. 141 and 77 on the east side of Kingsville, head south on Hwy. 77. Be sure you have plenty of fuel and water, as there are no services for the next 70 miles The chaparral and shrub-covered country will give you an idea of how empty Texas can be. Even when you top a small hill, there will be no sign of man for as far as the eye can see in any direction. From Kingsville, it is 103 miles of high-speed road to the turn-off onto Hwy. 100.

This road turns into freeway as it works through the built-up areas of Harlingen and San Benito. Exit onto Hwy. 100 and turn left toward Port Isabel. You are now only 25 miles from the most famous and best-developed beaches in Texas, South Padre Island. Along this ride you will leave the more developed and drier areas and again encounter marshlands. The high-rise condominiums on the island are visible on the horizon many miles before you get to them. Take the two-mile long bridge that connects Port Isabel with South Padre Island and make the first left turn. All the upscale hotel chains have property here and it seems the condos run for miles. There's everything you can imagine in a top-notch resort destination: you can buy a T-shirt, get a tattoo, rent a dune buggy or motorcycle, parasail, jet ski, or charter a fishing or sail boat. There is even a gambling boat that goes out for evening cruises. A few miles up this road the development thins out and you are again riding along remote beautiful beaches and sand dunes.

Tonight you have the option to stay either on South Padre Island, as described above, or in Port Isabel. If you choose **South Padre Island,** let your budget be your guide. By getting off the beach only a block or two, you'll find major chains, like **Motel 6** and **Days Inn** with rooms in the $75 range (these prices can double or triple during high season, on the weekends, or during special events). The rapid increase in land values and new development has left very few "mom and pop" places on the island. Most of these rent cottage-type accommodations with kitchens to families spending their annual week-long vacation on the beach. Campers will find the **Isla Blanca County Park** (956-761-5493) located on the south end of the island to be handy to the action.

Port Isabel is a much older and more picturesque town than South Padre Island. Although it has more permanent inhabitants (5,000 vs. 2,000) it lacks hordes of tourists. The **Port Isabel Lighthouse State Historic Structure,** on your left at the end of town near the bridge entrance, is hard to miss. Once a vital navigational aide to mariners, the lighthouse is still in operation today. It is open to visitors and the view from the top is grand, overlooking the development on South Padre Island and the surrounding waterways.

Originally a fishing village that is still operational, Port Isabel has several motels in the moderate to inexpensive range. The **Yacht Club Hotel** *(Sandy's Choice)* at 700 Yturria Street (www.portisabelyachtclub.com, 956-943-1301, $125) has great ambiance, as it is a restored 1920s fishing lodge. Dining options are plentiful and there is no shortage of great seafood. The dining room at the Yacht Club Hotel, considered the best place in town, offers the sort of upscale dishes that one would not expect to encounter in a town this size. It is reasonably expensive, but the cost is offset somewhat by the fact that your room rate includes a continental breakfast.

Day 4   Port Isabel to Laredo

Distance *235 miles*

Features *This day is a real mixed bag of riding, starting out with a run along the seashore, you'll soon be heading through the immense farmlands of the Rio Grande Valley. The day ends with miles of open spaces covered with mesquite, cactus, and scrubs. Take the time to visit an old Spanish mission and view what was once the northernmost port on the Rio Grande.*

At the intersection of Hwy. 48 with Hwy. 100 in Port Isabel, turn left onto Hwy. 48 toward Brownsville. This stretch is unusual in that on your left will be sand dunes covered with sea oats—a typical beachfront road; on your right, however, will be a desert landscape of cactus and scrub. It is as if the road serves as a climatic barrier.

The old lighthouse in Port Isabel still leads ships home. It is a very popular motorcycling destination and the view from the top is extraordinary. (courtesy of TxDOT)

PORT ISABEL LIGHTHOUSE
STATE HISTORIC STRUCTURE
TEXAS PARKS & WILDLIFE DEPARTMENT

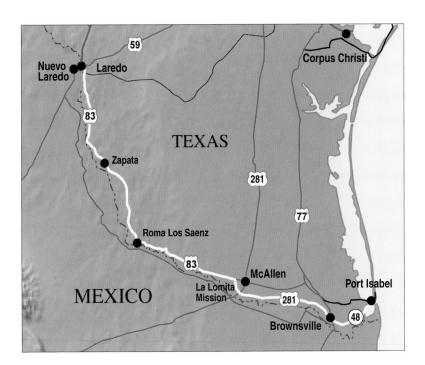

Continue on Hwy. 48 for 23 miles. The road will become a four-laner as you approach **Brownsville** and it can get quite congested during rush hours; after you go under Hwy. 77, traffic will clear out some. At the intersection with Hwy. 281, continue straight (do not turn onto Hwy. 281 Business).

Your proximity to the Mexican border and the high percentage of Hispanic residents in the area is evident in the fact that almost all outdoor advertising is in Spanish. In fact, Brownsville has more Spanish TV channels than English ones.

The next 50 miles or so on Hwy. 281 run through the heart of the Rio Grande Valley with its enormous farms being worked by migrant laborers. Climatic conditions produce a year-round growing season. The highway, a major truck route that conveys goods from Mexico, is a good, high-speed road that curves gently as it roughly follows the route of the **Rio Grande River.**

Just before the town of Hidalgo, the signs indicate a right turn onto Hwy. 281 north; do not make this turn, but continue straight ahead as the road turns into Hwy. 281 west. About two miles past this intersection, turn right onto Hwy. 336. To stay out of the congestion of McAllen, turn left onto Hwy. 1016 after about 4 miles. You will now find yourself riding through sugar cane and sorghum fields.

Side Trip

Approximately 6 miles down Hwy. 1016, turn left at the sign for **La Lomita Mission**. Just a few hundred yards down the road, the right turn to the mission will be clearly marked. Cross the railroad tracks and make a left. The mission will be ahead on your right in a small grove of live oak and mesquite trees.

The **La Lomita Chapel** is located in a small, restful park. It was originally built in 1865 as an adobe overnight waystation for padres traveling between Brownsville and Roma. This tiny structure was rebuilt in 1889 of sandstone. Today it has been carefully restored and contains the original brick floor and heavy overhead wooden beams made from the nearby trees. A beehive oven and the well are also still in existence. Today the place is still used for special events, such as weddings, and locals come here to pray and light candles. When you are ready to return to the road, retrace your route and turn left when you intersect with Hwy. 1016.

Only two short miles down the road from the La Lomita turn-off, turn right onto Hwy. 83. The next 50 miles to Roma Los Saenz is all four-lane and you can make good speed through this fertile valley of aloe vera, onions, cabbage, and various other vegetables. From that point, you will come upon mile after mile of rolling chaparral thick with mesquite trees and prickly pear cactus. In Roma, turn left at the traffic light just past Lino's Pharmacy.

These days, **Roma Los Saenz** is just a sleepy border town, but from 1850 to 1900 it was a bustling seaport, being the westernmost point on the Rio Grande open to steamboats. It was vital to the South during the Civil War as an export point for cotton. The left turn described above will get you down to the river and into the heart of the historic district, which contains more than 38 restored structures. Since it so well resembles a typical small Mexican town of the era, the outdoor scenes for the movie *Viva Zapata* were shot here. After visiting the river and the historic district, return to Hwy. 83 and turn left.

From this point, Hwy. 83 turns into a two-laner and traffic really drops off. The terrain becomes hillier and from the tops of the rises you can see forever over the mesquite—and cactus—covered countryside. The 40-mile run to the town of **Zapata** is about as desolate as it gets in the United States. If you love moving along open road on two wheels, this will be pure heaven. If you need fuel, tank up in Zapata, since the 48 miles to Laredo consist of more of this wonderfully deserted country.

The quaint La Lomita Chapel sits in a restful grove of live oaks near McAllen. Established in 1865, it still is in service today.

As you approach Laredo, Hwy. 83 reverts to four-lanes, makes a quick 90-degree turn to the left and becomes Guadalupe Street. Continue onward toward Salinas and turn left at the blue sign that indicates TOURISTS TO MEXICO. Turn left on Lincoln Street, and in two blocks you will see the visitors' center on your left at the corner of Lincoln and St. Augustine. I recommend you stop here to pick up brochures and maps of the **Laredo Historic District** and information on visiting Mexico, as well as discount coupons for some of the hotels in the area.

If at all possible, consider spending two nights in Laredo so you can really experience this very interesting place. For a real treat, try *(Sandy's Choice)* the **La Posada Hotel & Suites** at 1000 Zaragoza Street (www.laposadahotel.com, 956-722-1701; 800-444-2099). Deluxe rooms will cost you $170 and up, but the last time I was through here, the visitors' center had coupons for a $69 rate. If you make reservations let them know

Migrant laborers play a major role in harvesting the vast fields of produce in the Rio Grand Valley. (photo by Tx/DOT)

you will be arriving with a coupon. Sitting on the Rio Grande River, this hacienda-style hotel has nice courtyards filled with vegetation and flowers. It is located between the two international bridges and is within easy walking distance to both the historic district of Laredo and the tourist district of Nuevo Laredo. Some of the higher-priced rooms have patios overlooking the river into Mexico. It also has a very good river view restaurant.

I can't recommend the lower-priced hotels and motels in downtown Laredo. If you are seeking reasonably priced accommodations, head north on I-35 and you will find several "budget" chains, including a **Motel 6** ($55). The only camping in the Laredo area is in **Lake Casa Blanca State**

Park. As the name would imply, the campsites are on the lake. Three options exist: sites without water, sites with water, and screened sites. To get here, take I-35 north to the Hwy. 59 east exit. Stay on Hwy. 59 and the park will be on your left just past the airport.

Laredo is a city of approximately 250,000 people, 90 percent of whom are of Hispanic heritage and almost 40 percent are less than 21 years of age. The language heard most often on the streets and markets is a mixture of Spanish and English called "Spanlish." Laredo's economy revolves around trade between the United States and Mexico, and it is the largest port of entry between the two countries. With the advent of NAFTA and the subsequent *maquiladora* factories, Laredo has become the second-fastest growing city in the country (Las Vegas is first).

For the visitor, Laredo consists of the downtown historic district. You will feel as if you are south of the border, with street vendors hawking traditional Mexican foods from their carts, walkways cluttered with wares, and rampant bargaining.

Located right next to La Posada Hotel & Suites is the **Republic of the Rio Grande Museum,** which has exhibits concerning the short period of time after the Texas War of Independence that the Laredo area was an

The fertile Rio Grande valley provides much of the citrus found in your local supermarket. Here you can "pick it up at the factory." (photo by Richard Reynolds/TxDOT)

In south Texas, a little Spanish can come in handy.

independent republic. From here, you can catch an air-conditioned trolley tour of the rest of the historical district; sit back, relax, and let a guide explain what you are seeing. A brochure at the visitors' center also outlines a walking tour of the historic district. The oldest section of Laredo is around **San Augustín Plaza,** just across Zaragoza Street from the hotel. Several cobblestone walkways leading from it provide welcome shade and places to just sit and watch the goings on.

Just a short stroll across **International Bridge #1,** you enter into Mexico and the city of **Nuevo Laredo.** As of this writing a birth certificate and driver's license is the only identification required to go over and spend the day. However, this is in a rapid state of change and a passport or equivalent documentation may well be required in the near future. Please check the current requirements before leaving home. It is highly advised that you have your passport with you even if it should not be required (you do want to come back, don't you?). As you enter Mexico, the road becomes Guerrero Avenue and the next nine blocks along this busy street to **Plaza Hidalgo** will really give you a feel for the differences, as well as the similarities, of these twin cities. Nuevo Laredo is the larger of the two, with an estimated population of 400,000.

Be sure to stop in the **Mercado Juárez** on your right, just after Calle

Belden, to see a typical Mexican market in operation. As a general rule, the closer you are to the border, the more expensive the food will be, as these establishments are geared to the tourist trade. On the south side of Plaza Hildalgo, the **Café Lanchería** serves up Mexican (not Tex-Mex) dishes at reasonable prices. As always in Mexico, drink only bottled beverages. The merchants in Nuevo Laredo usually accept U.S. dollars, but it is fun to change a few dollars into pesos at the bridge so you can use the local currency. You can change back any leftover pesos on your return.

A few words of caution: As with border towns everywhere, petty crime here is fairly high, though if you are alert, you should have no problems. Authorities in both cities understand the value of the tourist trade, and as a result, violent crime is almost non-existent. That said, avoid carrying large sums of cash in the historic district of Laredo and the tourist district of Nuevo Laredo and do not walk along unlit streets at night. Park your bike in a secure area with 24-hour protection.

During your visit to Nuevo Laredo, you will likely encounter people on the street offering to sell you all sorts of goods and services, some legal, some not. Try to remember that these folks are usually just trying to make a living the only way they can. A grin and a friendly, "No, gracias," should be enough to send them on to the next prospect. Should you ever feel uncomfortable, just walk over to one of the many policemen who will be around and tell him of your problem.

Do not under *any circumstances* carry a weapon, or even ammunition into Mexico, unless you would enjoy a lengthy stay in a Mexican jail. Knives are considered weapons, and it is best to leave your pocketknife in your hotel room. For some excellent tips to make your crossing painless, pick up the *Crossing Guide for Los Dos Laredos*, a brochure available at the visitors' center. Go and enjoy the experience!

Day 5 Laredo to Goliad

Distance *200 miles*

Features *Leaving the rugged terrain of south central Texas, you will encounter farmlands and pass through several oil fields with their associated equipment dotting the landscape. As you approach Goliad, the landscape becomes wetter and more lush with trees and vegetation. Since tomorrow will be a full day of riding, try to get to Goliad in time for some sightseeing this afternoon.*

Since the first part of today's ride is through some fairly desolate country, be sure your tank is topped off and you have a good supply of water with you before you depart the city. From San Augustín Plaza, head north on any street until you reach Chihuahua Street and then turn right (this runs parallel to your route into the city, but in the opposite direction). The street will make a 90-degree turn to the right and become Hwy. 83. Just after this point, take a left onto Hwy. 359.

After you depart the outskirts of Laredo, you will find yourself again in open country. The road has gentle hills and an occasional sweeper that

In south Texas, fine examples of old Spanish missions remain in active service today.

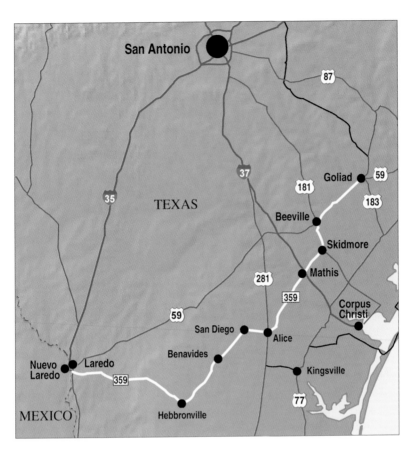

seems to last for miles. After approximately 43 miles, you'll reach the town of **Hebbronville,** where Hwy. 359 makes a right turn, and then an almost immediate left turn, and one block later another left turn (all of which are clearly marked). It is now approximately 65 miles to the town of Alice. Just follow Hwy. 359 signs through the virtual ghost town of **Benavides** and make the clearly marked right turn in San Diego. Enjoy these miles, as after this you will be back into "civilization."

When you arrive in **Alice** (pop. 20,000) you will have left the brush country to the west and re-entered the coastal plains and farm country. Alice is located only 29 road-miles from Kingsville and was named after one of Captain King's daughters. From 1888 to 1985 it was the world's largest cattle shipping point. Oil was discovered in the area in the 1930s and remains the primary business today. Alice is considered the dividing line between the border regions and the rest of Texas. Hwy. 359 takes off to the left in Alice, and you will be on a rural, two-lane road again.

The Empresario restaurant in the small town of Goliad is the best place to eat in town.

Hwy. 359 runs through mostly farm and pasture lands for the 26 miles to **Mathis,** where you will begin to see trees again. This area produces large quantities of grain sorghum, flax, and oil. Follow the signs for Hwy. 359 in Mathis and continue onward. Should you wish to get a taste of Africa, make a stop at **Wayne's World Safari,** located about one and one-half miles on Hwy. 359, after the intersection with I-37. Covering more than 50 acres, this wildlife park contains more than 300 animals, including tigers, bears, lions, zebras, monkeys, and many more species, all roaming freely on the plains.

Continue on Hwy. 359 for approximately 13 more miles and turn left onto Hwy. 181 north in the town of **Skidmore.** The next 12 miles of four-lane road present a very dramatic change in scenery. Turn right off Hwy. 181 in **Beeville** onto Hwy. 59 toward Goliad. As you ride the 28 miles to Goliad, the terrain becomes hillier and the road has a few interesting curves. More and more, as the roadside becomes more forested, you will realize that you have left the coast behind.

As you enter Goliad, the **Antlers Inn** (361-645-8215, $50) will be on your right. This is the best place to stay in town, although there is another budget motel ahead at the light. There are several fast food options and the **Hunter's Café** at the hotel serves adequate food. By far the best place to eat in town is the **Empresario Restaurant** located on the town square. Unfortunately, it is open for dinner only Thursday through Saturday nights. Try it for breakfast anyway. To get to the square, follow signs for the historic district, with its historical markers and old buildings. A huge oak tree, known as "**the hanging tree**," earned its moniker during the years following the Civil War, when a group of men known as The Regulators filled the vacuum left behind by a lack of organized law enforcement. With no trials, justice was swift and the sentences were predetermined by these men.

Campers should continue to the intersection with Hwy. 77 Alternate/ 183 and turn right. About two miles down this road, the **Goliad State Park** will be on your right, with both primitive and improved sites, as well as toilets and shower facilities.

The small town of **Goliad** (pop. 2,000) sits among live oak groves on the banks of the **San Antonio River.** One of the oldest settlements in Texas, it recently celebrated its 250th birthday. While it is now just a sleepy little ranching town, it was once a major cattle center larger than San Antonio. As

Walking the streets of many small Texas towns today will make you feel as if you are on a western movie set. (photo by Bob Parvin/ TxDOT)

Galveston gained ground as the main port in Texas, Goliad declined. Hollywood has ensured that most people are familiar with the Texican battle cry, "Remember the Alamo!" but an event that took place in Goliad was actually an even more stirring factor in fueling Texican resolve to win independence from Mexico.

After the defeat at the Alamo, Texican colonel **James Fannin** was ordered to withdraw his troops from the fort in Goliad and join up with Sam Houston's forces in the east. Shortly after leaving the fort, Fannin and his men encountered a superior Mexican force and surrendered honorably as prisoners of war. On March 27, 1836 (Palm Sunday), **General Santa Anna** ordered all 350 of these men to be executed by firing squad; the bodies were stripped and left unburied. Such an atrocity inflamed the Texicans, and when they encountered the enemy later at San Jacinto, the slaughter continued for more than two hours after Mexico attempted to surrender, accompanied by cries of, "Remember Goliad!"

The fort, **Presidio La Bahia** was originally established by the Spanish to protect the **Mission Nuestra Senora del Espirtu Santo de Zuniga**, which had become a major ranching center for Texas. Located just south of town on opposite banks of the San Antonio River, these two sites have been carefully restored and are open to the public. The fort, the size of a city block, is considered the best surviving example of the Spanish presidios. You are free to roam the interior and visit the small museum containing artifacts and

These shaded roads cast a very different picture of Texas after you've spent a few days in the wide-open spaces.

The Presidio La Bahia in Goliad makes for an interesting visit to explore Texas roots.

other memorabilia from the Texas Revolution. Located in **Goliad State Park,** just across the river, the mission has also been restored and contains exhibits outlining the daily life of the padres and the Indian converts during its 110-year history as an active mission. To get to these sites, just go south out of town for about two miles on Hwy. 183/77 Alternate.

Day 6   Goliad to Houston

Distance *240 miles*

Features *This day offers a real contrast to everything you have experienced so far. Most of the day consists of hilly, curvy roads that can be ridden as aggressively as you want. The old town of Gonzales, the birthplace of Texas Independence, makes for a nice lunch stop. Your day ends with a high-speed run through miles of rice fields as you approach Houston.*

The old jailhouse in Gonzales now serves as a museum and headquarters for the local travel bureau.

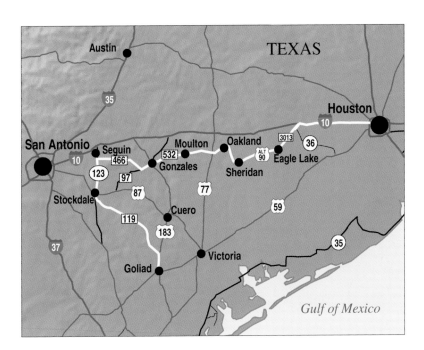

From the intersection of Hwys. 59 and 183/77 Alternate, head north toward Cuero on 183/77 Alternate for approximately nine miles, and then turn left onto Hwy. 119. The next 58 miles are full of gently rolling hills and curves meandering through pastureland and live oak tree groves. Settled by people of European descent (mostly Lithuanians), there's relatively little evidence of Hispanic culture in the area.

As you come to the town of **Stockdale**, take a left onto Hwy. 87 at the T-intersection and about a quarter-mile later, turn right onto Hwy. 123. The next 20 miles or so consist of good high-speed riding on a somewhat larger road than before.

Turn right onto Hwy. 477. After about two miles, Hwy. 477 ends at the intersection with Hwy. 1117, and you should proceed straight to pick up Hwy. 466, which is part of the **Texas Independence Trail.** You can easily imagine settlers with horse-drawn wagons traversing this hilly landscape and camping along the sides of the streams. You may even have to reduce your speed to navigate the curves.

After approximately 27 miles of pure riding pleasure, turn left onto Hwy. 97. Go five miles, and then turn left onto Hwy. 183. In about two miles, take a right onto Hwy. 183 Business in Gonzales (the sign also indicates the historic district).

Known as the **"Lexington" of Texas,** the first shots fired in the War of

Large rice storage and transporting facilities sprout out of the otherwise flat marshlands as you approach the sprawl of Houston.

Independence were discharged in Gonzales. When the Mexicans demanded that the townspeople give up their small cannon, they refused, and fought under a hastily made banner that said, "Come and Take It." Thirty-two men who made a mad dash to the Alamo to help in its defense lost their lives. As he began his retreat to San Jacinto, **Sam Houston** ordered the town evacuated and burned to the ground.

After the war, **Gonzales** was rebuilt and it became an important ranching area. Old cotton plantations and majestic homes along tree-lined boulevards have been carefully maintained. The old jail constructed in 1887 on the main square has been restored, complete with cells, dungeon, and gallows. The chamber of commerce located here can provide you with a map for a short ride around the town to see the more impressive old homes.

After visiting downtown Gonzales, continue on Hwy. 183 Business to the intersection with Hwy. 90 Alternate and turn right. Only two miles down this road, make a left turn onto Hwy. 532, which is a road any motorcyclist will enjoy. After about 18 miles on Hwy. 532, turn right in the town of Moulton, make another right as it joins Hwy. 95, and a left just a short way down this road, and then another left (all these turns are clearly marked).

Over the next 15 miles, the road opens up somewhat and you might be tempted to twist the throttle, as you have good visibility through the turns. Be on the lookout, as there are several 90-degree curves along here and if you are riding at high speed, they can sneak up on you. You should make a right turn as Hwy. 532 joins with Hwy. 77 for a short distance before leaving it to the left toward Oakland.

Turn right onto Hwy. 155 at the T-intersection. Eleven more miles will place you at the end of Hwy. 155, where you need to turn right onto Hwy. 90 Alt. The next 11 miles are on a major state highway through a vast rice growing region. There are several wildlife refuges through here and many migratory birds winter in the area. The small town of Eagle Lake is the self-proclaimed **Goose Hunting Capitol of the World.**

Shortly after passing through **Eagle Lake**, take a left onto Hwy. 3013, for a straight 17-mile shot to the intersection with Hwy. 36, where you should turn left. Take I-10 east just south of Sealy and 45 miles later you will be back in Houston at the intersection with Loop 610. Having passed through nearly 20 miles of ever-increasing development with subdivisions, shopping malls, and even some modest skyscrapers just to get to this "outer loop," gives you an appreciation for just how huge Houston has become.

The banner says it all about the attitude of Texicans during the War of Independence from Mexico. If you want this cannon, "Come and take it!" (photo by Jack Lewis/TxDOT)

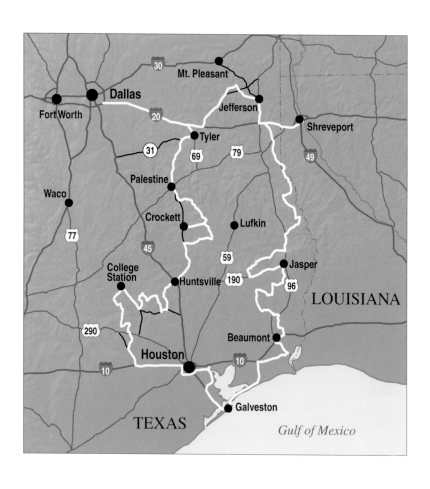

East Texas

Forget any preconceived ideas you may have about Texas. East Texas is very different from the rest of the state, with an abundance of thick forests, rivers, bayous, and lakes. The flat coastal marshes and grasslands turn into gently rolling hills as you head north. This chapter details six days of riding, covering approximately 1,280 miles, starting and ending in Dallas. All the routes described here are paved, but the four national forests through which you will travel and the Big Thicket National Preserve contain a maze of dirt roads that offer hour after hour of backcountry riding.

Culturally, east Texas also moves to its own beat and you will see fewer folks in cowboy hats and boots. East Texas was primarily settled by people from the southeastern United States: cotton farmers and second sons of old families from Georgia, Alabama, and Mississippi. Since this was the only area of Texas to hold significant numbers of slaves, today's population has a larger percentage of blacks than other rural parts of the state. Its distance

Huge lakes surrounded by piney woods are liberally sprinkled throughout east Texas.

Evidence of the oil industry will be all around you as you ride the Texas gulf coast. This semi-submersible drilling rig is headed for offshore waters to continue the search for resources and riches. (photo by Randy Green/ TxDOT)

from Mexico has mitigated Texas's otherwise heavy Spanish heritage. Instead, the earliest history of Texas was influenced by the French; a Creole and Cajun heritage spilling from neighboring Louisiana still can be found in the local accents, food, and style.

From a rider's point of view, east Texas is a delight. Roads seem to go in every direction, twisting and turning through the forests and piney woods. Except for along the coast, this area is relatively undeveloped. The residents are more laid-back, and the abundant opportunities to enjoy regional food will more than likely put a few inches on your waist before you leave. The architecture of the buildings and homes in these small, scattered towns resembles that of New Orleans. Oil and lumber are the primary industries, though tourist dollars are helping to cultivate an appreciation for the unique history of the area.

Dallas-Fort Worth and the surrounding suburbs have the largest population of any area in Texas. From a standard metropolitan area measurement viewpoint, the "metroplex" contains more than 6,100,000 people, and covers an area of more than 9,200 square miles (larger than the states of Rhode Island and Connecticut combined). Dallas is the larger of the two cities, and can claim approximately 1,250,000 citizens within its limits. The Big D also has more shopping area per capita than any other city in the nation. These people like to spend their wealth and show it off. By comparison, Fort Worth (Cowtown, USA), with a mere 650,000 residents, trails far behind in population. While Fort Worth has money in its own right, the people seem to care less about what the world thinks of them and are less ostentatious in their lifestyles.

Dallas was founded in 1840 on the **Trinity River** with the building of one log cabin that served as an area trading post. It slowly grew over the years, but ranching, farming and the usual small town Texas economy never developed. Trading remained the lifeblood of Dallas. In the early 1870s, two rail lines were extended to Dallas, and the town grew. Although cattle were not driven to Dallas, cattle futures were traded there. When oil money from other parts of Texas came to Dallas to be "put to work," the area became a center for banking and insurance. Today it is the home of many Fortune 500 companies, as well as a center for the high-tech and aviation industries. As a result of this diversity, Dallas considers its economy virtually "recession proof."

Fort Worth was established as an army camp in the 1850s, but a small group of settlers soon built cabins around the camp for protection from the Indians. After the Civil War, when the great cattle drives from Texas to Abilene, Kansas, began, Fort Worth was the last place to get provisions and supplies on the way north; heading back south, it was the first place the cowboys could spend their money and have a good time. Think of all those Westerns that depicted cowboys riding their horses up and down the streets shooting their guns in the air, drinking, gambling, whoring, and having just a generally rowdy time. This was Fort Worth.

When the railroad reached town in 1876, Fort Worth became the endpoint of the drives and vast cattle yards and feedlots were built. Gradually, over the years, improved transportation and refrigerated transport led to the construction of many packing plants here, and the need for the stockyards decreased. Today, Fort Worth has transformed itself into a fully modern city, and is the home of American Airlines, Bell Helicopter, Pier One Imports, and numerous other national and international companies.

With the exception of man-made "green belts" the Dallas-Fort Worth area sits on a vast plain with few trees. It is not a rider's dream. However, the **Dallas-Fort Worth airport**, larger than the entire island of Manhattan, is one of the busiest in the world. Since flying into the Dallas area from anywhere in the world is easy, and rental bikes are available (see Appendix A2), I chose to start and end this chapter here. In a little more than 100 miles of high-speed riding, you will be enjoying wonderful roads through the piney woods of east Texas.

Obviously, these two cities offer the full range of lodging options; all chains are represented with multiple locations. Having said this, *Sandy's Choice* is the Rosewood Mansion on Turtle Creek, 2821 Turtle Creek Blvd. (www.mansionatturtlecreek.com). Starting at $300, call 888-rosewood, if you dare.

Both Dallas and Fort Worth can brag of world-class museums of all types, but there are some sights unique to these cities that you might care to visit:

Southfork Ranch. You can visit the location where the famous TV show *Dallas* was filmed in the '70s and '80s. This series was responsible for branding a whole generation with the notion that Texans and Texas oilmen were as devious as **J.R. Ewing**, with his "anything is O.K. for me, because I am rich" attitude. Today the site displays memorabilia, including "the gun that shot J.R." It is a very popular stop for visitors today, many of whom still have trouble separating fact from fiction. (www.southforkranch.com, 800-989-7800 for more information and directions)

The Kennedy Legacy. On November 23, 1963, President John F. Kennedy was shot and killed near Daley Plaza in downtown Dallas. Against the advice of some of his closest advisors, Kennedy chose to make the trip in hopes of bolstering his sagging political fortunes. The many theories surrounding the assassination are enough to keep you reading for a lifetime. Located on Elm Street, a small museum on the sixth floor of the **Texas School Book Depository** (214-747-6660; www.jkf.org) outlines the life, death, and legacy of JFK. You are even able to look out the window from which **Lee Oswald** made his shots. Take a stroll over to the infamous "grassy knoll" and draw your own conclusions. An auto tour using the same type of limousine in which JFK was riding passes the spot where he was killed and plays recordings of radio reports from that day as it covers the ground to the hospital.

Texas Cowboy Hall of Fame. Located in an old horse and mule barn at 128 E. Exchange Avenue in the Fort Worth Stockyards National Historical District, the Cowboy Hall of Fame celebrates the life and times of Texas

The swamps and bayous in east Texas amaze many a rider with preconceived ideas about this state.

cowboys who have excelled in the sports of rodeo and cutting. Twenty-seven individuals are honored with displays of photos, memorabilia, and audio-visual presentations concerning their exploits and accomplishments. A special section of the museum gives tribute to the famous boot maker, **John Justin.** Although he arrived in Dallas virtually penniless, he became a multimillionaire through hard work and determination, building the largest boot factory in the world. Later, Justin generously gave back to his beloved Dallas, both in monetary donations and through serving in many civic capacities.

The antique wagon display may seem a little out of step with the rest of this facility, but it is an interesting visit nonetheless. There are more than 60 wagons on display, including a Sicilian cart from the 1750s with intricate iron work and painted scenes, and a Welsh funeral hearse complete with beveled glass windows, gold leaf paint, and plumes. (www.texascowboy-halloffame.com, 817-626-7131)

Texas Cowgirl Hall of Fame. This museum is the only one in the world dedicated to honoring and documenting the lives of women who have distinguished themselves while exemplifying the pioneer spirit of the American West. The current 159 honorees not only include cowgirls and ranch women, but also writers, artists, and teachers who made their mark on the

Many of the rides on this route run along the Texas Forest Trail. Enough said.

settling of the west. Honorees include **Narcissa Prentiss Whitman** (the first woman to cross the Rockies), as well as the renowned artist **Georgia O'Keefe**. Located at 1720 Gendy Street (817-336-4475; www.cowgirl.net).

Fort Worth Stockyards and National Historic District. The complex, located at the site of the original stockyards at 131 E. Exchange Avenue, includes some of the original pens. Although it is an active cattle exchange, most of the trading is done via satellite today. You are welcome to sit in on one of the auctions, but be careful about moving your hands and feet or you might end up going home with a steer!

As the stockyards declined and development crept into the area, the U.S. Department of Interior made the entire complex into a National Historical District in 1976, to prevent future "improvements." Today, it's home to nearly 50 livestock commission companies, in addition to numerous other offices (mostly attorneys and architects). The district is dotted with saloons, restaurants, western wear stores, and just about anything you can think of pertaining to the cowboy and his life.

Texas Justice

Texas history is steeped with outlaws, savages, and invaders that have always been met with swift and harsh justice. The Texas Rangers were known for their ruthlessness in handling Indians, Mexicans, and outlaws. The U.S. Army protected much of Texas for a time and handled offenders as do most armies: the suspected lawbreakers were rarely tried.

After the Civil War, carpetbaggers from the northern states poured into Texas to line their pockets at the expense of the general population. Groups of ordinary citizens, called Regulators, took it upon themselves to bring order and punish criminals. These vigilantes held sway for several years until decent state law enforcement was re-established. In Goliad, the "hanging tree" on the town square says all that needs to be said about their methods.

Today, justice in Texas follows the rest of the nation in adhering to constitutional rights, and the legal system is consistent with other states. However, Texas Rangers still have a reputation for being rough and tough when faced with apprehending criminals. They also enjoy the well-earned reputation of being some of the best in the business.

When faced with today's Texas judges and juries, a criminal learns first-hand the general attitude of the public regarding punishment. Prison sentences are most often set to the maximum possible and the "hanging tree" is still used frequently (although now it is a lethal injection). Since the death penalty was reinstated, Texas leads the nation by far in its number of executions. If you plan to break the law, choose a different state.   ✪

The **Fort Worth Visitor Center** (817-624-4741), across the street from the Exchange building, can supply you with a wealth of brochures and maps to get you on your way. They even offer walking tours of the entire complex several times a day.

Day 1 Dallas to Crockett

Distance *230 miles*

Features *The good stuff will begin after a stretch of high-speed riding over open prairie to get out of Dallas. Consider a stop in Tyler, the Rose Capitol of America, and a visit to the oldest Spanish mission in east Texas, reconstructed on its original site.*

From the intersection of Loop 635 and I-20 on the east side of Dallas, take I-20 east for 89 miles; take Exit 556 onto Hwy. 69 and head south, toward the city of Tyler. After nine miles, you will intersect with Loop 323 on the

A visit to this restored, failed Spanish mission in east Texas can give real insight to the struggle for land rights between the original French and Spanish settlers.

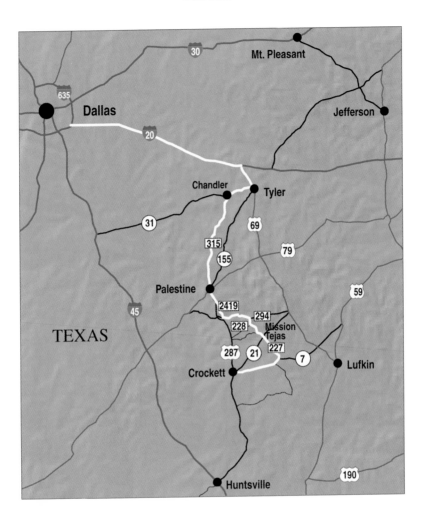

outskirts of Tyler. Turn right and follow Loop 323 for two miles to the intersection with Hwy. 31 (Front Street). If you care to visit the Municipal Rose Garden Visitors' Center and Museum (see below), turn left here and just follow the signs for a few short blocks. If you do not wish to make this stop, turn right here.

The city of **Tyler,** with a population of more than 80,000 is by far the largest city in northeast Texas. It is called the **Rose Capitol of America,** and rightly so, as it provides more than 20 percent of the rose bushes sold in the country. Growing, displaying, and selling roses is the number one industry here. This industry supports the local tourist business with thousands of people descending on the city for the famous **Tyler Rose Festival** held during mid-October each year.

Lumbering is big business in East Texas. Keep an eye out for debris left on the road. (photo by TxDOT)

Side Trip

Roses are in bloom May through October, and are proudly on display at the **Tyler Municipal Rose Garden** located at 420 S. Rose Park Drive. Covering more than 14 acres, the garden contains over 30,000 bushes of seemingly endless varieties. Adjoining the garden is the **Tyler Rose Garden Center and Museum.** If you have the slightest interest in flowers in general, and roses in particular, this can make for a wonderful stop, even when the plants are not in bloom. After your visit, retrace your route and continue west on Hwy. 31.

Follow Hwy. 31 for seven miles and turn left onto Hwy. 315 in the town of Chandler. While Hwy. 31 is a major highway, the views of all the lakes and woodlands beside the road make it quite worthwhile. After turning onto Hwy. 315, get ready for 41 miles of absolutely wonderful motorcycle riding, as few roads this good exist in the world. The road is typically in good shape, so if you want to take the rpm's up, enjoy. At slower speeds you'll have time to wish it all would never end. This may be the best motorcycle road in all of east Texas.

Turn right onto Hwy. 155, and a very short distance later, turn left onto Loop 256 to stay on the outskirts of Palestine. After five miles, turn left onto Hwy. 287. Another five miles later, turn left onto Hwy. 2419, proceed 11 miles, and turn left onto Hwy. 294.

After departing **Palestine**, the roads become smaller again with the limbs of the trees often draping over the entire roadway. After 15 miles on Hwy. 294, turn right onto Hwy. 228. Three miles later, turn left onto Hwy. 3016; in another five miles or so, turn left onto Hwy. 227. Four miles later, turn right onto Hwy. 21.

Side Trip

At the Hwy. 21 intersection, turn left and 1-1/2 miles later the **Mission Tejas State Historical Park** will be on your left. This is the location of the first Spanish mission built in east Texas to aid their efforts of stopping the intrusion of the French. Originally established in 1690, it has a colorful history of abandonments, destructions, and reconstructions over the years. It was finally relocated in 1730. A replica of the mission was built in the 1930s and is open to the public today. The setting is one of rustic beauty and tranquility common to the east Texas piney woods. If you are camping, sites are available with water and showers. It makes a great site on which to end the day.

After visiting the park, retrace your route and pick up Hwy. 227, which runs concurrently with Hwy. 21 for about a half-mile before veering off to the left. Take this turn. This is a delicious motorcycle road for the next 13 miles. Turn right onto Hwy. 7, proceed 21 miles, and turn left onto Loop 304 in the small town of Crockett. The **Crockett Inn**, located at 1600 Loop 304 east (www.crockett-inn.com, 936-544-5611, $60) will be on your right just down the road. This motel, while somewhat overpriced, is really the only decent place to stay in the area. It does have an excellent restaurant with fresh homemade bread to enhance your waistline.

Day 2 Crockett to College Station

Distance *210 miles*

Features *This day offers more opportunities to ride the east Texas woodlands and enjoy this countryside so close to Houston. You can also visit the Texas State Prison in Huntsville and see the "World's Largest Statue to an American Hero." Some of these roads today will be as good or better than you have ever ridden.*

At 65 feet in height, this statue of Sam Houston just outside Huntsville is truly "larger than life."

From the Crockett Inn, retrace yesterday's path on Loop 310 and turn right onto Hwy. 7. After 16 miles, continue through the small town of Kennard, and about a half-mile past the yellow blinking light, proceed straight ahead onto Hwy. 357.

After 11 miles, go straight ahead and pick up Hwy. 233. Another five miles down the road, turn right onto Hwy. 358. Thirteen miles later, turn left onto Hwy. 2781 in the town of Pennington. Follow this road for seven miles and turn right onto Hwy. 1280.

In another eight miles, turn left onto Hwy. 19. You will have been riding the backroads of the **Davy Crockett National Forest** all morning. While the roads are not very dramatic through here, they are nice, traffic-free rides through the country and woods. The next 34 miles on Hwy. 19 will be more open and prone to higher speed. Turn right onto Hwy. 30 and you'll enter the town of Huntsville.

The city of **Huntsville**, with a population that exceeds 20,000, is most famous as the home of the **Texas Department of Criminal Justice**. With seven prisons that can house up to 13,690 inmates at any given time, this is Huntsville's most important industry. The department employs nearly 7,000 people.

The Raven—Sam Houston

The first president of the Republic of Texas, Sam Houston was the earliest in a long line of colorful, controversial, and illustrious Texas politicians. Born in Virginia in 1793, his family soon moved to Tennessee. As a youth, he ran away from home because he didn't like to work or go to school and lived with the Cherokee Indians for more than three years. These Indians called him The Raven, and the name stayed with him for the rest of his life.

Tiring of the Indian lifestyle, Houston returned to civilization and read for the law. He joined the army and soon became a protégé of Andrew Jackson. After practicing law for a while, he soon found his true calling in politics, serving as governor of Tennessee. Houston served three terms to the U.S. House of Representatives before returning to live with the Indians.

In 1832 Sam Houston moved to Texas for unknown reasons, possibly for land speculation, maybe as a U.S. agent to urge entrance into the Union, or, perhaps, to help establish an independent nation. Whatever his original intentions, he soon became a major figure in the Texas fight for independence and subsequent operations of the new nation.

Houston was a signer of the Texas Declaration of Independence and was named as commander-in-chief of the Armies of Texas during that fight. He led his men to victory over Santa Anna at San Jacinto and was soon elected president of the Republic.

Because of Houston's size and reputation as a heavy drinker, he was called the Big Drunk. He was re-elected president in 1841. After Texas joined the Union, Houston served as a U.S. senator and later, as governor of the state. His career was doomed, however, by strong stands in favor of Indian rights and his pre-Civil War opposition to succession from the Union. His third wife, a highly religious Baptist woman, influenced him to quit his heavy drinking and move to Huntsville as a private citizen, where he died.

It's hard to determine what is fact or fiction among the many stories that circulate about this man. That he was a natural-born leader, had amazing abilities to govern despite his personal problems, and is a true hero in the hearts and minds of the people of Texas is about all of which we can be sure.   ✪

Texas justice is harsh. The state more often than not leads all states in the number of executions each year (Florida is usually second, but did beat out Texas one year). In 1997, there were 37 executions here. In total, nearly 600 people have lost their lives at the hands of the state in Huntsville.

To get a look at the original prison, built in 1849, turn left onto Avenue I; as you enter town on 11th Street, you can circumnavigate the complex. There is even a **Texas Prison Museum** at 1113 12th Street, that includes taped interviews of people who have since been executed; the original electric chair, **"Old Sparky;"** various items confiscated from prisoners over the years; Bonnie and Clyde's rifles; and more. You can even "visit" a 9 x 6 cell.

After returning to 11th Street, turn left, continue to the county courthouse, and turn left onto Sam Houston Avenue. **Charlotte's Ribs & Thangs** located at 2530 Sycamore and Sam Houston Avenue offers some of the best barbeque available anywhere. Approximately five miles down this road, you'll spot the "typically Texas" **World's Largest Statue to an American Hero** on your left. Of course, it honors Sam Houston.

If you reach the interstate, you have gone too far. To best view the 67-foot statue, park your bike at the visitors' center and take a short stroll down the pleasant wooded path. There is plenty of information in the visitors' center about Huntsville and the prisons, including a suggested driving tour of the city and the system.

Return to Hwy. 30 (11th St.) and turn left. Continue west on Hwy. 30 for about five miles, then turn left onto Hwy. 1791. Follow this pleasing road for 17 miles and then turn left onto Hwy. 149. The speed limit on Hwy. 149 is 55 mph; if you ride the speed limit, this will be one of the most enjoyable touring rides of your life. If you care to ride this road at 70 mph, you have a super sport-bike road.

After about 12 miles, turn right onto Hwy. 105 in **Montgomery**. After five more miles, take another right onto Hwy. 1486. Fourteen miles later, turn left onto Hwy. 2819 toward Anderson. Just before getting to Anderson, there is a fork in this road with no numbers indicated; take the right-hand fork with the sign pointing to **Anderson**.

Ten miles after getting onto Hwy. 2819, turn right onto Hwy. 90, proceed a mere two miles, and turn left onto Hwy. 244. Six miles later, turn left onto Hwy. 3090. For the next 10 miles you can ride this delightful road at as high a speed as you want, but be alert, as it contains some serious curves that can sneak up on you.

After these 10 miles, follow Hwy. 3090 off to the right, proceed another six miles, and turn right onto Hwy. 6—a high-speed, four-lane road that is not, however, an interstate. Stay on the lookout for crossing and entering traffic. After 19 miles, exit left onto Hwy. 6 Business. As you enter **College Station,** home of **Texas A&M University,** you will see signs welcoming you to "Aggieland."

There are almost unlimited places to stay and eat along this road. A good, basic place to stay on the edge of the campus is the **E-Z Travel Motor Inn** (www.eztravelinn.com, 888-354-5822, $65) at 2007 Texas Avenue S. (Hwy. 6 Business) with a good steak house and barbeque place next door. Several other dining options are within walking distance. As this is a university town, your choice of watering holes is almost boundless.

Actually there are two towns, College Station and **Bryan.** If it weren't for the city limit signs, however, you wouldn't know the difference. The permanent population is estimated to be something like 70,000. But don't let this mislead you. The 50,000 students of Texas A&M University swell the local ranks each year.

The university is the overriding driving force in the economy and the social life of the cities. The Texas A&M campus covers more than 5,000 acres and a more loyal and fervent student body, alumni, staff, and followers will not be found anywhere on the planet. Originally established in 1871 as an agricultural and mechanical college (hence the nickname "Aggies"), it was originally an all-male school with required military training until 1964—the year the first women ("Maggies") were admitted. Military training then became optional.

Today the "Corps" has an enrollment exceeding 2,000 and they make quite a sight in football game parades. Today, the world-class university contains 10 colleges covering all courses of study. The **George H. Bush Presidential Library and Museum,** located on campus, details the life and accomplishments of this former president, and is an oft-visited site by outsiders, as well.

The University of Texas vs. Texas A&M

The state of Texas contains many fine universities. The two largest, each with several campuses throughout the state, have student populations approaching 100,000. Both the main campuses, University of Texas at Austin and Texas A&M at College Station, boast student populations of about 50,000. These two world-class schools have received awards for academic excellence, and graduates from each usually go on to successful careers in many fields.

These two schools project different cultures and each is fiercely proud of its own. The University of Texas is considered the more sophisticated of the two. Students and alumni are often referred to as "Tea Sippers" as a reflection of their social graces. Texas A&M was originally founded as an agricultural college and their loyalists are called "Aggies." A line in one of the schools fight songs further enhances this image, "Fight, Farmers, Fight." As with any generalization, these images no longer hold true to form on either campus.

Students and alumni from the two schools co-exist peacefully during most of the year, working side by side, doing business together, attending the same churches, and sharing the same neighborhoods. However, it is still considered somewhat of a social blunder to seat graduates from the two schools side-by-side at a formal dinner or reception.

The armistice comes to a halt each year around Thanksgiving, when the two football teams face off on the gridiron. No matter the record of either team, the pride and honor of each school is on the line. It reminds one of the Civil War, in that it pits brother against brother, husband against wife. Business partners take their respective sides and friends quit talking to one another the week building up to the battle. Taunts are hurled, practical jokes abound, and bets are placed not so much to reflect the actual expected outcome of the game, but purely as a matter of honor. The game itself reminds one of war, as both teams rise to the occasion and give it their all.

A few days after the game, things begin to return to normal until the next year. As a visitor to Texas, enjoy the hullabaloo. To stay out of the fray, it is best to keep your mouth shut, as fans of neither school will believe anyone could be neutral on such an important issue. ✪

Day 3   College Station to Galveston

Distance   *235 miles*

Features   *This day starts off on mostly flat rural roads alongside farms and pastures, but a few curves and sweepers can make for some fun. You'll loop around the megalopolis of Houston and then take a backroad route to some of the most hallowed ground in the state of Texas, see a large inland lake containing one of the world's largest collection of yachts, and visit the NASA headquarters.*

Backcountry roads with little traffic meandering through thick woods will have you stopping often!

From your motel, go to the intersection of Hwy. 6 Business and Hwy. 60 on the north side of the campus. Turn left onto Hwy. 60, a four-lane ride for 14 miles. Turn left onto Hwy. 2155 and follow it for six miles. By now, you will have left the city and are once again on nice country motorcycle roads.

If you wish to see a small farming town typical of this area, take a right on Spur 2155 as you approach Snook; in a few short blocks it will take you back to Hwy. 2155, where you'll turn right. At the intersection with Hwy. 1361 turn left.

After three miles on Hwy. 1361, turn right onto Hwy. 50, a main highway that nonetheless makes for a very enjoyable ride through pasturelands and farms. Nineteen miles later, turn left onto Hwy. 105, a major four-laner, but you will only be on it for six miles. Turn right onto Hwy. 2193. The next 27 miles of riding will be your last chance on this route to enjoy rural roads, so slow down and enjoy them.

After three miles on Hwy. 2193, turn right on Hwy. 1155 and eight miles later, at the T-intersection, turn left onto Hwy. 1371. At the STOP

The more than 1,000 restored Victorian mansions in Galveston are enough to attract many visitors. (photo by Richard Reynolds/TxDOT)

sign, go right onto Hwy. 1371, proceed seven miles, and turn right onto Hwy. 1456 toward Bellville. After nine miles take a left onto Hwy. 36; in about 15 miles you will intersect with I-10 east, only 45 miles from the intersection with Loop 610 in Houston. The ride into Houston will give you a good idea as to just how large this city really is. Development extends over 20 miles before you reach the "outer" loop.

Alternate Route

If you have the time, consider exploring the sights in the Houston and Galveston area; these are outlined below and discussed in more detail at the beginning of the Coastal Route chapter. If you have to keep it moving, and can't take the time to see the sights this time around, you could go directly to the intersection of I-45 south from Loop 610. I-45 south will take you directly to Galveston from there.

Turn south on Loop 610 and follow it around town to the intersection with Hwy. 225 east.

Traffic on the freeway system in and around Houston is usually heavy. Hang in there and stay alert as you navigate your way out of town. You will soon go through the towns of Pasadena and Deer Park. Most people are overwhelmed the first time through here by the sights and smells of the massive crude oil refineries and petrochemical plants that line this road.

After 11 miles, exit onto Battleground Road (Hwy. 134) and follow signs to the San Jacinto Monument, a pilgrimage Texans take quite seriously. Just 2-1/2 miles up the road, turn right to the battleground and monument.

The **San Jacinto Historical Complex** is located on the site where the Texicans defeated **General Santa Anna** and his army to secure their independence from Mexico. Leaving the battleground, follow the signs directing you to the permanent mooring of the **battleship Texas**, the last surviving battleship to serve in both World War I and World War II. It has been extensively renovated and is open for tours. From the battleship you can get a close look at the huge tankers carrying crude oil, petroleum products, and petrochemicals in and out of the ship channel.

After your visit to the San Jacinto Complex, retrace your route on Hwy. 134 to the intersection with Hwy. 225 and turn left. After four miles, turn

This seawall was constructed after a hurricane in 1900 wiped out Galveston. The city never regained its former prominence as the major city in Texas.

Luxury resorts and world-class accommodations are in plentiful supply in Galveston, just bring money.

right (south) onto 146. From this point, you will still be in an urban area, but the traffic thins to some extent and you can give your nerves a rest. After nine miles you'll need to take a right onto NASA Road 1 in **Clear Lake,** a wonderful sheltered cove for yachts and boats of every description, with access to the Gulf of Mexico via **Galveston Bay.**

Six miles along NASA Road 1, you'll see the **Lyndon B. Johnson Space Center** on your right, mission control for all NASA space operations. To see the facility, you must first visit **Space Center Houston,** located on your right about a block past the NASA entranceway. Interesting exhibits and films outline the U.S. space program, and some of the original spacecraft are on display. Trams to the NASA facility itself operate on an almost continuous basis. You could spend a whole day here.

The quickest and easiest way to reach your destination of Galveston Island is to continue on NASA 1 until the intersection with I-45. From there, head south for approximately 28 miles until you cross the bridge onto the island. As you travel along this road, the traffic thins, and you will soon be in a rural area of vast marshlands. After crossing onto the island, the road becomes Broadway (Avenue J); continue straight ahead until you reach the ocean.

After passing though some fairly seedy neighborhoods, you'll be approaching the ocean, and Galveston's restored Victorian homes will brighten your outlook. When you can see the ocean, turn right, to put yourself on Seawall Blvd. (for some reason, this intersection is marked as 6th Street).

There is a good selection of motels and hotels in Galveston in every price range. A good medium-priced place to stay is **Gaido's Seaside Inn** located at 3802 Seawall Blvd. (www.gaidosofgalveston.com, 409-762-9626, 800-525-0064, $90). As everywhere, a room with an ocean view commands a premium; you can save about $20 if you don't mind a view of a parking lot. Note also that the fenced, locked parking area for these rooms is quieter and more secure than the one facing the seawall.

Gaido's restaurant, next to the inn, is deemed by many to be the best place to eat on the island. **Casey's Seafood Restaurant,** located in the motel, has the same fare at a much lower price, as it has the same owners and operators as Gaido's.

The nearest camping to the city of Galveston is about six miles southwest off Seawall Blvd., on 61st S.E. at **Galveston Island State Park** (409-737-1222, $20). This is a beautiful setting with nature trails that go from the ocean on one side to the bay on the other. Galveston State Park accepts reservations and the facilities include flush toilets, showers, grills, and picnic tables.

Check the **Galveston Convention and Visitors Bureau** at 2106 Seawall if you are interested in touring the many Victorian mansions. For $1, a trolley will take you through **The Strand** and **Silk Stocking,** two of the historic districts.

To get an idea of how the rich of Galveston lived during its heyday, visit **The Grand,** the opera house built in 1894. Located at 2020 Post Office, it is a magnificent building. Self-guided tours are available of the interior. It is true opulence.

The **Bishop's Palace,** located at 1402 Broadway, will be on your left as you enter Galveston. The **American Institute of Architecture** has designated this Victorian structure as the second most impressive in the United States. Original in every detail and carefully preserved, tours are offered daily. If you plan to see only one of these homes, this should be it.

Day 4 Galveston to Jasper

Distance *205 miles*

Features *This day offers a nice mix of riding. Starting out on the ocean, a nice ferry ride brings you to flat marshlands with a Cajun flavor. In Beaumont, you can visit Spindletop and an interesting Harley-Davidson dealership with its next-door H.O.G.G. House. Sweepers and low hills surrounded by heavy woods and bayous bring the day to an end in a fisherman's mecca.*

Your food choices change dramatically after the Bolivar Ferry crossing.

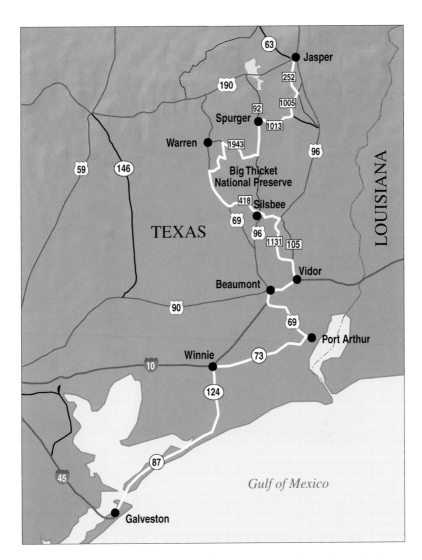

Return back east on Seawall Blvd. and turn right onto Hwy. 87 (at the intersection where you turned right yesterday to get onto Seawall). In just a
block or two, turn left at the sign indicating the ferry landing.

As you approach the loading area, you more than likely will see a long
line of vehicles waiting their turn to load. As is the rule at most all ferries,
motorcycles can go to the front, as they can load in spaces autos cannot. Ignore the signs about no passing or cutting in and continue to the front of
the line. Unfortunately, some motorists do not understand or appreciate
this practice, and you may be subjected to some horn honking and hand

gestures. However, be assured you are doing what is correct and expected.

The **Boliver Ferry** is free and takes about 15 minutes to make its transit, time well spent watching for marine life and gazing at the array of ocean going ships passing by or at anchor waiting for dock space.

Almost immediately after leaving the ferry you will notice that you are in an entirely different culture. In this flat marshland, people speak with a Cajun accent, eating places go from offering barbeque and chicken-fried steak to specializing in crawfish etouffee, shrimp gumbo, smoked boudain, and other Cajun delicacies. After debarking, continue on Hwy. 87 for 28 miles and then turn left onto Hwy. 124.

Alternate Route

At the time this book was written, Hwy. 87 was closed past Hwy. 24 due to hurricane damage. My efforts to obtain estimates as to when, or even if, it will be repaired received mixed, confusing, and unreliable results. The following directions assume this highway will remain closed and routes you on to Port Arthur another way. If you find that Hwy. 87 has been reopened, I suggest you take it.

Continue on Hwy. 124 for 21 miles and turn right onto Hwy. 73 in **Winnie.** Between the ferry and Winnie, the route is mostly flat and straight, through marshlands, though you will have an occasional view of the ocean and bay. For an interesting rest stop, check out one of the many bird sanctuaries along the way. One of the most pleasant, a place called **High Island,** is located on your left shortly after getting on Hwy. 124. Although this spot is less than 100 feet high, it was used as a refuge by early settlers during hurricanes.

As you approach Winnie and gain some elevation, you'll be riding through large rice fields. Winnie is the self-proclaimed **Rice Capitol of Texas.** On Hwy. 73, expect 30 miles of four-lane, high-speed road. In Port Arthur turn left onto Hwy. 69.

Fourteen miles on Hwy. 69 will have you in Beaumont. Take the Highland Avenue Exit and the **Spindletop/Gladys City Boomtown** and **Lucas Gusher Monument** will be on your right. You can explore a reproduction of the boomtown that grew up near the site of the first Spindletop well. A fifty-eight foot, pink granite monument commemorates the well alongside recreated examples of the original wooden drilling rigs. Several of the buildings in town are furnished in the era.

After your visit, turn left out of the parking lot, go one block and turn right, go to the first traffic light and turn right. This will bring you back to

The massive swamps and bayous found in East Texas are a surprise to many a rider. (photo by Stan A. Williams/ TxDOT)

Hwy. 69, where you should turn right. Continue on Hwy. 69 for four miles to the intersection with I-10. Take I-10 east to the first exit (College), go under the freeway, and turn left onto the frontage road. It will be impossible to miss the huge Harley-Davidson sign.

Cowboy Harley-Davidson (www.cowboyharley.com, 409-839-4464) and the adjoining H.O.G.G. House are sights not to be missed! This dealership looks out of place in Beaumont, Texas. You might expect something like it in Beverly Hills or Palm Beach. With more than 50,000 feet of display area housing over 200 motorcycles and all accessories known to man, the inside of the building matches the magnificence of the exterior.

The **H.O.G.G. House** next door was built by the dealership and is home for the local Harley Owners Group, which has more than 300 current members. It has a very upscale interior and all the comforts of home. Even if you are not a Harley fan, it's worth a stop, and everyone is welcome at the clubhouse.

After your visit, get back on I-10 east for 10 miles and take Exit 861A in **Vidor.** Go under the freeway and head north on Hwy. 105. Continue on Hwy. 105 for four miles and turn left onto Hwy. 1131. This 15 miles of road will be an introduction to the woods of east Texas, full of sweepers and curves alongside thick forests. Enjoy.

The Cowboy Harley dealership in Beaumont is well worth a stop, if only to gawk.

Turn left onto Hwy. 105, go one mile, and turn left onto Hwy. 96 toward **Silsbee**. After five miles on Hwy. 96, exit onto Hwy. 96 Business/418. Follow the frontage road to the T-intersection and turn right, following the signs to Hwy. 418. After only a half-mile, turn left onto Hwy. 418, a nice little road that meanders through the forest with gentle sweepers. After 11 miles, turn right onto Hwy. 69, a major four-laner that makes up for its lack of challenge in beautiful views. Seven miles later, turn right at the signs indicating the **Big Thicket Visitors' Center,** which will be on your left almost immediately after making this turn.

The area that makes up the **Big Thicket National Preserve** was, until after the Civil War, a vast, thick forest containing many rivers, bayous, and sloughs. Neither the native Indians nor the white man had attempted to penetrate or settle it. It did, however, serve as a haven for draft dodgers, out-laws, and runaway slaves, as they could literally "get lost" in its more than 5,000 square miles.

After the war, the lumber industry started to harvest the massive amount of timber in the Big Thicket. In 1974 it was made into a national preserve to protect what remained of this natural wonder; today it includes more than 100,000 acres. The Big Thicket has been called "America's Ark" and the United Nations has placed it on its list of **International Biosphere Reserves Worth Protecting**. It has diverse flora and fauna not found anywhere else in the United States.

The helpful staff at Big Thicket Visitors' Center have some excellent bro-chures outlining the scientific aspect of the park, even if most people are content with just gawking at the woodlands. If you are on a dual-sport bike, pick up the excellent map of delightful dirt roads in the area. A brochure outlining a half-day auto tour tells you of sights along the loop and is also applicable for those on street bikes.

Primitive camping is allowed in the preserve, but a free permit must be obtained at the visitors' center first. Because areas around the preserve are still being harvested, be on the lookout for the many log-carrying trucks on the road. They leave a lot of loose bark and other debris in their wake. Make sure your face shield is down when meeting or approaching one.

Leaving the visitors' center, return to Hwy. 69, and turn right. After four miles, you'll have to decide whether to continue on pavement or face a little bit of dirt. If dirt, take a right turn onto Hwy. 3063 (this is by far the more interesting route). When I was last through here, the roads were in good shape and could be ridden comfortably on a street bike. After about three miles, turn left onto Hicksbaugh Road, and three miles later turn right onto W. Midway Road. The dirt section ends eight miles fur-ther on, when you turn right onto Hwy. 1943. At the T-intersection with Hwy. 92, turn left and follow the rest of the route from there. This ride through the heart of the **Turkey Creek Unit** of the Big Thicket is wonder-ful and I recommend it highly.

Alternate Route

If you do not wish to ride dirt, just continue four miles on Hwy. 69 to the town of Warren, and then turn right onto Hwy. 1943, a very pleasant motorcycle ride through the woods. In 16 miles, turn left onto Hwy. 92.

Riders of all makes are welcome to stop by the H.O.G.G. House in Beaumont. These friendly folks will make you feel right at home.

Suitable lodging is hard to find in the small towns around here. I recommend you continue on to Jasper: following 92 north for eight miles, turn right onto Hwy. 1013 in the town of Spurger, proceed 10 miles, and then turn left onto Hwy. 1005. After 10 more miles, turn left onto Hwy. 252 toward Jasper. After seven miles, turn right onto Hwy. 190 into Jasper.

The **Best Western Motel** at 205 W. Gibson (409-344-7767, $80) is a more than adequate place to stay. It will be on your right as you enter town. Next to the motel, **Elijah's Café,** serves up heaping plates of down-home Southern cooking. There are several cheaper independent motels in town, but I don't recommend them.

If you prefer a more rural setting and are not on a tight budget, turn left onto Hwy. 190 and less than a mile later, turn right onto Hwy. 63. After eight miles, turn right onto Hwy. 255, proceed another five miles, and turn left onto Hwy. 1007. You will be three-quarters of a mile from the reception area for **Rayburn Country Resort** (800-882-1442, 409-698-2444, $95), complete with a 27-hole golf course. It is located on **Lake Sam Rayburn** and sits on a 3,000-acre patch of piney woods. Although the price for your room is not much more than downtown, the food, while good, is expensive.

Expect a tab for dinner to approach $25.

If you are camping, turn left when you intersect with Hwy. 190, go 12 miles, and then turn right onto Park Road 48 to **Martin Dies, Jr. State Park,** truly a wonderful setting on the banks of B.A. Steinnagen Lake. There are some screened shelters available and all campsites have water. For reservations, phone 512-389-8900.

Jasper, a town of approximately 9,000 people, is self-proclaimed as the **"Jewel of the Forest."** While the town was founded in 1860, it was completely destroyed by a fire in 1901. Jasper was rebuilt almost entirely of brick buildings, and you can stroll the downtown district in a short time. The people here are very proud of their town and make great efforts to make visitors feel welcome.

Outdoor activities attract most visitors to Jasper: camping, hiking, observing nature, and enjoying the wonderful lakes nearby. Fishing is big sport, and several professional bass tournaments are held here every year. The motels go so far as to designate parking places to accommodate a pickup truck with attached 20-foot bass boat (your motorcycle will look lonely).

Day 5 Jasper to Jefferson or Shreveport

Distance *To Jefferson: 175 miles; to Shreveport: 195 miles*
Features *This is a superb day of riding on some very good roads with many opportunities to stop and take in the natural sights. As a final destination, you'll have two very different choices: Shreveport, for a night of bright lights and gambling, or Jefferson, a sleepy old restored Southern town that will make you think you are in the bayous of the coast during the 1870s.*

Leave Jasper on Hwy. 190 west. The next 20 miles of high-speed road is a visual delight, especially in the spring when wildflowers line the sides of the roads. The many lakes and bayous containing giant cypress trees draped with Spanish moss run contrary to most folks' image of Texas. After this run, turn right onto Hwy. 256, every rider's dream road running through the forest with gentle hills and numerous sweepers. Very fast riding is not safe, as deer are plentiful here and your line of sight is limited by the heavy vegetation.

The fishing is good in the swamps and bayous found in East Texas.
(photo by John Suhrstedt, TxDOT)

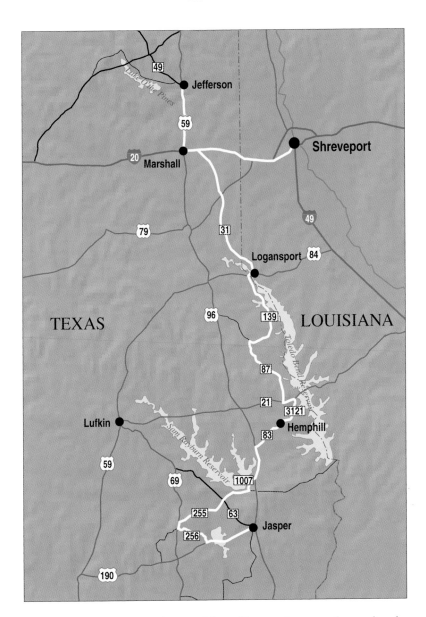

After 13 miles, turn right onto Hwy. 69, go only two miles, and make another right turn onto Hwy. 255. For the next 19 miles, you can pick up your speed, as the sides of the highway have been cleared back a good distance and you can see through the curves. Turn left onto Hwy. 1007, proceed five miles, and turn left onto Hwy. 96.

For the last few miles, you will have had some excellent views of the **Sam**

Rayburn Resevoir, the largest lake in Texas, covering more than 114,000 acres. It is thoroughly enjoyed by fishermen and utilized for all water sports, which can add a lot of interest to your rest stops. The road also passes the dam that created this lake—truly an engineering marvel.

Eleven miles up Hwy. 96, turn right onto Hwy. 83, and follow signs as the road works its way through the small town of Hemphill. You may have noticed by now that the further north you get in east Texas, the more frequent and pronounced the hills become. Five miles out of Hemphill, turn left onto Hwy. 3121, go another five miles, and turn left onto Hwy. 21. Five miles later, turn right onto Hwy. 87, a major road that is, nevertheless, a delight to ride. Although you are now going through the **Sabine National Forest,** some of the land along the road has been developed to pasture. After 16 miles, turn right onto Hwy. 139.

Slow down and enjoy the next 25 miles on Hwy. 139, as this is just about as good as it gets, with lots of hills, curves, and beautiful views. Turn right onto Hwy. 84 and cross the **Sabine River** into Louisiana at **Logansport.** Almost immediately after crossing the river, turn left onto Hwy. 169, proceed three miles, and then turn left onto Hwy. 31, which will take you back into Texas. Follow Hwy. 31 for 38 miles to the intersection with I-20—a pleasant ride with the potential for good speed.

Option

When you reach I-20 you must pick your destination for the evening. If you would like to try your hand at some riverboat gambling, head east to Shreveport. If you prefer a small quiet old southern town with an interesting historic district, take I-20 west.

If you're headed to **Shreveport,** just follow I-20 east for 39 miles. According to Louisiana law, all casinos must be on riverboats. It didn't take operators long to put the casinos themselves on permanent barges moored to the riverbank and build huge hotel complexes and support facilities on the adjoining bank. The two buildings are connected by covered "boarding walkways." In fact, you are given a "boarding pass" as you enter the casinos.

Almost all major gambling operators are represented off Exit 20, offering everything you would expect to find in Las Vegas. In addition to any losses your visit might incur, consider that the cost of the room will be around $100. Dining opportunities abound. A personal favorite, *(Sandy's Choice)* is the **Eldorado Resort Casino,** 451 Clyde Fant Parkway (www.eldorado-shreveport.com, 877-602-0711, $150). This place has it all to relax, eat, be entertained, and have fun while losing your money. If you want to gamble,

Small country roads seem to go in every direction. What a shame, so many roads, so little time.

but would rather not spend so much on a room, continue to Exit 21 and check out the **Motel 6** ($40). The cab ride back to the casino will only be a buck or two.

If you're headed to **Jefferson**, take I-20 west for only a mile or two, exit onto Hwy. 59 north, and go about 19 miles. As you enter the city, turn right onto Taylor to get into the historic section of the city.

For a city its size, Jefferson has an amazing array of places to stay. If you prefer a standard motel unit, try the **Inn of Jefferson**, located on your right as you come into town, at 119 S. Wolcott (www.hotel-jefferson.com, 903-665-3983, $65), a new motel within walking distance of the historic district. The **Excelsior House** at 211 W. Austin *(Sandy's Choice)* has been in continuous operation since the 1850s (www.theexcelsiorhouse.com, 903-

Old mansions tell of east Texas' southern heritage and of the cotton plantations that once existed here.

665-2513, $85 and up). Located at the center of things, the hotel's interior has been faithfully restored and furnished in the period. Should you wish to stay in one of the town's many historic Bed and Breakfasts, contact Jefferson Reservation Service (www.jeffersonreservationservice.com, 887-603-2535). Try the fresh seafood, Cajun and Creole dishes at the **Black Swan** on 210 Austin. The helpings are abundant and the price is moderate.

There are no camping facilities in Jefferson proper. Fortunately, there are plenty nearby that are excellent. Try **Johnson Creek Park** located on **Lake o' The Pines**, which is operated by the Corps of Engineers (903-755-2435). There are 22 campsites sitting in a beautiful rural setting in the pines beside the lake. Facilities include flush toilets, showers, and grills. To get there, take Hwy. 49 west out of town, turn left onto Hwy. 729 for 15 miles, and go south on the park road for one mile.

Located on **Big Cypress Bayou**, the town of Jefferson was once a major river port that boasted a population of more than 20,000. Steamboats from the Mississippi River would come up the Red River through **Caddo Lake** and on up the Big Cypress Bayou to load and unload cargo. It was dubbed the "**Gateway to Texas.**" During the Civil War, Jefferson exported cotton from the southern states. After the Civil War, it served as the jumping off point for many settlers headed further west. The vast timber resources of east Texas went through Jefferson on their way to market.

Jefferson became a river port because of an act of nature: the New Madrid earthquake created a massive log jam on the Red River, known as the "**Great Raft,**" that raised the water levels in Caddo lake and the bayou, allowing steamboat traffic. It is no longer a river port due to an act of man: in 1873, the U.S. Corps of Engineers removed the Great Raft, lowering the water levels. This change, along with the construction of railroads into Texas, led to the town's rapid decline.

Today, Jefferson is a sleepy little town of 2,500 people. Its gorgeous setting and the efforts of its residents to restore the town as it was in its glory days do attract visitors, however. Many antebellum homes and business establishments have been brought back to their former grandeur. Trolley tours, walking tours, boat rides, and even mule-drawn carriage cover the downtown historic district, making tourism the number one economic influence in the area today.

Day 6 Shreveport or Jefferson to Dallas

Distance *From Shreveport: 249 miles; from Jefferson: 177 miles*
Features *This day offers some truly world-class twisties through the piney woods. Visit downtown Jefferson and take note of the old plantation homes on the sides of the roads.*

If you spent your evening in **Shreveport,** gather up all your winnings and get back on I-20 west and take Exit 633 (the second exit after you re-enter Texas) onto Hwy. 134 north after 26 miles. Eleven miles along this road, turn left toward Jefferson in the middle of a 25 mph curve marked with flashing yellow lights. For the next 10 miles, the riding is as good as it gets, traveling over hills and around curves through the forest.

Do you ever wonder what is around that next curve?

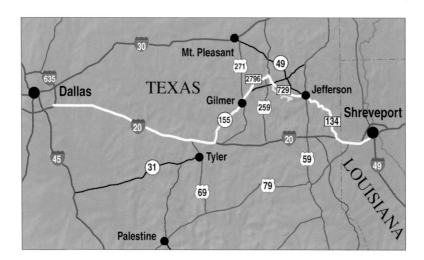

Turn right onto Hwy. 43, go 11 miles and turn left onto Hwy. 134. There are several restored plantation homes along Hwy. 43 to remind you that this was once a cotton-growing region. Fourteen miles on Hwy. 134 will have you in Jefferson.

If you spent your evening in **Jefferson,** take the time to spend the morning exploring this delightful town. Leave town on Hwy. 49 west, ride five miles, and turn left onto Hwy. 729 for 23 miles of serpentines through the woods. Don't let the wool gather, as this stretch does have a few curves that will get your "pucker factor" up if you're not paying enough attention.

Turn left onto Hwy. 259, a major four-lane road on which you will travel only three miles before turning right onto Hwy. 557. Most of the three miles on Hwy. 259 is elevated and goes over a swamp. After about a half-mile on Hwy. 557, turn left onto Hwy. 2796, proceed 11 miles, and turn right onto Hwy. 155, which goes off to the left after about eight miles in the town of Gilmer. Continue on Hwy. 155 for 27 miles of enjoyable motorcycle riding, and then head west on I-20. A quick 100 miles will have you back at your original starting point at the intersection with Loop 635 in Dallas.

Introduction to Mexico

Mexico is an exciting country that can be as exotic as any destination on earth; yet it sits on our southern step. The two trips in this section, each about a week long, will introduce you to the northern interior of Mexico. Also included is a short history, details of the customs and habits of these wonderful people, entrance requirements, and other tips to make your trip easier and more enjoyable. Perhaps after testing Mexico you will want to return again and again, as we have, to enjoy even more. Other routes (and adventures) into Mexico are outlined in my *Motorcycle Journeys Through Southern Mexico.*

Many riders are reluctant to ride into Mexico. Tall tales (mostly unsubstantiated) of past experiences, sensationalized press reports, and rumors fuel these unfounded fears. Please take all these with a grain of salt. I personally have traveled over 100,000 miles by motorcycle in Mexico over many years and while I have had many an adventure, I have had no negative experiences to compare with what I have encountered while riding along the byways of the U.S.

Are there unusual conditions in Mexico that require special attention? Of course! Do they require some unique types of caution and care? Of course! Are the rewards from these efforts worthy of your time and effort? Absolutely!

Go, ride, taste, live, and enjoy Mexico!

General Information

Riding and traveling in Mexico is different than riding and traveling in the U.S., but that does not mean it is less safe. Customs and regulations differ from country to country so don't expect things to be the same as they are back home. One of the joys of traveling is seeing how other people live. Enter Mexico with an open mind and a desire to learn and you can be richly rewarded.

It is also important that you keep your good manners. Whether you wish to or not you are representing all Norte Americanas. You are also representing the motorcycling community in general. Don't be a bad example of either. I know it's hard, when you are hot, dusty, and tired, to try to be patient with that person who cannot fulfill your wants instantly. But remember, you are the one who is the stranger in a strange land, you are the one who cannot speak the local language, and you are the one that got yourself into this miserable situation, not them. You are a visitor; act like one. Let the memories you leave behind always be good ones.

A dual-sport rider can explore endless back roads in Mexico. (courtesy of MotoDiscovery)

ENTRANCE REQUIREMENTS

You are bringing two things into Mexico, yourself and your bike. You want to bring them both back. To do this you must have the proper paperwork ready to satisfy the Mexican authorities and law to enter and Homeland Security to return (unless you wish and your bike to remain stranded there). You will need a passport to get the necessary visitor's permit *(tarjeta de turista)* to enter the interior of Mexico for up to 180 days and then again to reenter the U.S. All persons entering must obtain this piece of paper. It must be surrendered upon your exit from the country.

Your bike is a more complicated situation. You are, in effect, entering your bike into the country without having to pay necessary tariffs (in bond) and promise it is only for personal use and to remove it from within the country within 180 days (don't sell it!). A bank *(Banjéricto)* actually handles this transaction instead of the Mexican government. You present a major credit card, it is charged a small fee ($25) and a $400 "hold" is made against it in the case you do not adhere to the terms of this transaction when leaving. Unless you enjoy seemingly endless hassle and trouble, remember to close this paperwork out when leaving the country. While this may seem complicated, it is not, thousands of motorcyclists enter Mexico each year without undue problems. Just remember that you will need the following: a) passport, b) driver's license, c) title and registration of the bike—*in your name,* and d) a major credit card in the same names as the passport, driver's license, title, and registration.

Unusual circumstances, such as you wish to take a friend's bike, the bank still has the title (God forbid), your girlfriend wants to pick up the tab (God bless her), will complicate this process somewhat, but almost all sets of circumstances can be handled if you do a little checking prior to arrival at the border. The easiest way to find the ins and outs of your particular situation is to do an internet search for "Mexico Temporary Vehicle Import Permit" and do some research. Also all the motorcycle tour operators for Mexico have excellent websites that address these issues.

The important thing to remember is: if you do not have the required documents, you will not be traveling into Mexico. Do your homework, round up the documents, and smile as you stand in line to get the procedure completed and then—enjoy.

INSURANCE

Your current insurance is not valid in Mexico! Now, don't panic, Mexican insurance is readily available. Rather than "suggesting" a particular company I recommend that you spend a few minutes on the internet before

Views like this one along the high desert make it hard to concentrate on the road.

leaving to explore your options. Proof of liability insurance is required to get the vehicle entry permit mentioned above. Coverage beyond that is hard to find. Try www.mexinsure.com for quotes/options. If you wish, liability insurance on a daily basis is readily available at most border crossings. I suggest that you get this detail out of the way before leaving home as most companies will issue a policy via the internet which you can print out and have with you.

Please note that the Mexican legal system differs from ours in that in Mexico you are presumed guilty until you are proven innocent. If you are involved in a minor accident, your proof of insurance is your "get out of jail free" card. Review your options carefully; purchase from a reputable company, then place this item out of your mind.

RIDING IN MEXICO

You will be riding along unfamiliar roads, sometimes in a crowded city; signage (when you can find it) will be in Spanish and you will also encounter some unusual road conditions. Yes, there may be cows on the side of the road or maybe on it, people tend to crowd up (watch out for bus stops) and seem unaware of your presence. In many locations a motorcycle is somewhat unusual and an unexpected vehicle. Drivers follow local rules and habits that may be strange to you. How do you handle all this safely? Slow down. Become a little more alert of your surroundings, always assume you do not have the right-of-way, and watch how others are driving. If you do these things, relax, and keep a good attitude with you, you soon can be riding along safely and at ease.

NAVIGATION

Road signs in northern Mexico are usually very good. Instead of using a highway number, Mexican road signs are usually labeled with a destination, much as they are in Europe. When entering larger Mexican cities, however, it can get very hectic. Signs will be in Spanish, people will be everywhere, and roads will double back on themselves without any semblance of a grid pattern. In these instances, I often use the "taxi trick" to lower my blood pressure. Just write the name and address of your hotel or the name of the central plaza on a piece of paper and put it in a handy place. When you are lost and have had enough, stop and show it to a taxi driver and ask to be led to your hotel. Make sure you determine the price beforehand—usually a buck or two. Obviously, you can use this same method to get out of a city and onto the main highway to your next destination.

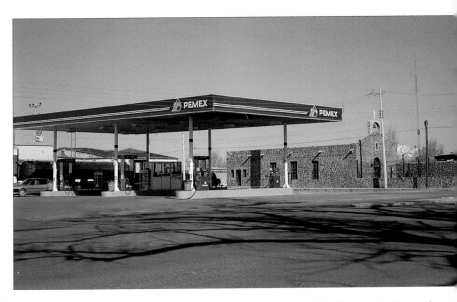

In northern Mexico, modern gas stations exist right alongside beautiful old stone churches.

A good night's sleep will be easier if your bike is inside a closed courtyard just outside your door.

MONEY

The Mexican unit of currency is the peso. It fluctuates on a daily basis and has currently been running about ten pesos to the U.S. dollar. You can get pesos at almost all border crossings, but if you run short while in Mexico, banks usually offer the best exchange rates, although their exchange service may only be available during the morning hours even when the bank is open in the afternoon. ATMs are available in major cities and they typically offer a great rate of exchange. Credit cards are useful at many locations, but don't count on hotels accepting them. PEMEX stations do not accept credit cards, so plan to use cash for your gasoline purchases. In more remote areas, *cambio* (change) is not always available. Try to keep several small-denomination peso coins available for these instances.

GASOLINE

The only service station you will find in Mexico is PEMEX. This is the government-controlled national oil company. As anywhere in the world, when the government gets involved, service usually deteriorates. While great improvements have been made in the past few years, gas stations can still be few and far between and they may have no supplies when you pull in. I recommend always running on the top half of your tank. When filling up, you may encounter an all-too-common scam I call "the 100-peso trick." If you owe less than 100 pesos and you give the attendant a 200-peso note, make sure he does not give you change for only a 100-peso note. When you gently remind him that you gave him a 200-peso note, he will "remember" immediately and give you the remaining change.

HOTELS

Mexican hotels differ from what you will find in the U.S. Unless they are in the "budget" category, you can expect them to be clean and have all the basic amenities. If you intend to stay in a lower-end hotel, be sure and ask if they have *agua caliente* (hot water), and have a look at the room before checking in. One thing you will notice at once is the lack of a washcloth in the bath. If this is important to you, bring one from home. Some of the hotels recommended in this book are very old and located on a busy central square; ear plugs can sometimes come in handy.

MEDICAL TIPS

Medical care and drugs are readily available in Mexico. In fact, many medicines that are only available by prescription in the U.S. can be obtained over the counter at a Mexican pharmacy (notice the ads for Viagra). Nevertheless, by bringing any prescription drugs you use regularly (in their original containers) you can save yourself much time and effort. Other common remedies readily found at home may not be available in Mexico (Rolaids, for example). Plan to bring with you a supply of anything you use routinely, as well as a few "emergency" items.

MOTORCYCLE REPAIR

I am continually amazed at the ingenuity and competence of Mexican "shade-tree" mechanics. Electrical and electronic problems can be difficult, but if you have a simple mechanical problem, they will figure out a way to get you back on the road. Generally in Mexico, few dealerships have repair facilities, so an independent repair shop will usually be your best bet. Most major cities will have a parts supply store that stocks an amazing number of parts for almost every common model of bike. When the mechanic determines the problem, he will send a runner to purchase the part. *¡No problema!*

Take along a few spare parts if you know beforehand that your model bike is prone to certain problems. If space allows, a spare chain or master link can often be a real ace in the hole.

CHOOSING YOUR BIKE

This is like the question of which bike is the "best." I usually travel in Mexico on a Kawasaki KLR 650 because it is reliable and simple to repair, and it gives me dual-sport capability. However, I have also traveled in Mexico on a Honda VFR and a BMW R1100RS. Do remember, however, the more complicated the machine, the more difficulty you're likely to encounter in obtaining repairs. In my opinion, all routes described in this book can be ridden on a heavy dresser. I point out a small number of dirt side trips for those who wish.

You can enjoy the view of a colonial church while relaxing on the porch of your hotel.

Green Angels

The *Secretaria de Turismo* operates a fleet of more than 1,000 trucks that patrol the major highways of Mexico to assist motorists with mechanical problems. These plainly-marked, green-and-white trucks usually have a two-man crew that is somewhat bilingual. They carry gasoline, oil, and other minor parts for on-road repairs, as well as a first-aid kit. They will be familiar with your route, know where the next service is, and have radio contact to get you the assistance you need. Although there is no charge for their services, you should offer a tip. If you are on the side of the road and can find a phone, call 91-800-90-392 to have the nearest crew sent to your aid.

I once threw a chain 70 miles from the nearest town. As I was standing on the side of the road with the sun setting, wondering what to do, and reluctant to leave my bike, the green-and-white truck pulled up. After we reviewed the options, they loaded the bike into the back of the truck and we proceeded to the nearest hotel. Since they were not satisfied with the parking security at the hotel, one angel who lived nearby insisted that he take my motorcycle to his house for safekeeping. The next morning, which was his day off, he came to the hotel and we went to an open-air market where he located a chain that would work. We then returned to his house where he installed the chain. He refused a tip. *¡Angeles Verdes!*

Mexican Customs and Habits

You travel to a strange country to see the sights, meet new people, and learn their ways. In Mexico, many things are different than they are at home.

EATING

This can be one of the great joys of traveling in northern Mexico. Don't expect to see what is available at "Mexican" restaurants in the U.S.; that is Tex-Mex, not true Mexican food. Most larger Mexican cities now have American chain restaurants. You will see the familiar Golden Arches, as well as Domino's pizza delivery motorcycles twisting through traffic. You will also find other types of "foreign" food in the larger cities (Italian, Chinese, etc.). I suggest you do not eat in any of these places unless you are homesick. You came here to see Mexico, you should taste it too.

Mexican eating opportunities run the full gamut, from the most elegant establishments to the most humble street vendors. Try to eat with the locals. A small cafe off the plaza will provide you with a great quantity of food at a reasonable price. Eating a freshly caught fish in a thatched roofed, four-table place looking out on the ocean can be a real pleasure. The folks at the *gringo* hotel a few miles down the road will be eating the same thing with none of the ambiance at four times the price.

Meal times in Mexico are a little later than those in the U.S. If you want to get on the road at 7:00 a.m., better get some sweets or fruit the night before as few places open before this hour. Lunch is generally taken between 1 p.m. and 3 p.m. and dinner starts after 9 p.m. If you choose to eat earlier, you will probably be eating alone or with other *gringos*. To a Mexican, a meal is more than just the food, it is an occasion that can take several hours to enjoy. Service will be slow as the food is generally prepared only after it has been ordered, and *la cuenta* (the check) will not be presented until you ask for it. (If your Spanish is poor, pretend to sign your palm; a few minutes later the check will appear.)

Since food selection and preparation reflect regional preferences, few general statements can be made regarding what you will find available. Obviously, when you are near the coast you can expect the seafood to be wonderful and fresh. *Pescado frito* is a whole fish fried well done. *Filete de pescado* (filet of fish) is also generally fried. An all-time favorite, *huachinago a la veracruzana,* is a grilled filet of red snapper covered with a red sauce and olives. Lobster tacos are often offered by street vendors near the sea, but these are best enjoyed earlier in the day when they are fresh.

You can eat your lunch on the plaza beside a mission church, which offers a glimpse into the past.

A staple of the Mexican diet is *frijoles* (refried beans), and they will be included with just about every meal, including breakfast. Unless you request *pan* (bread) when ordering your meal, expect to be served *tortillas,* thin, round, cooked cakes of corn or wheat flour. These little cakes are survival food for the poorest Mexicans, and with a little butter and salt they often make up an entire meal. It is unusual to find grain-fed beef offered in all but the very best eating establishments. As a result, beef will be tougher than what you are accustomed to. It is usually sliced very thin and cooked well done. Try the *bistec milanesa* which is similar to a "chicken-fried" steak in the U.S. To find out more about what else you might encounter, see On the Menu in the Appendix.

While in Mexico, order what you think you want and then wait for the surprise!

The television is a constant feature in small Mexican eateries and you can expect the volume to be full on!

DRINKING

Booze is readily available throughout northern Mexico. Domestic beers, wines, brandy, and the infamous tequila can be found in any town and often at roadside stands. Mexican drinking habits generally reflect the social status of the participants. At the top of society, men and women might have a glass of wine with their lunch at a high-class restaurant. At the bottom are the *cantinas* where women are not welcome and the rear wall often serves as the restroom. Unless you are adventurous, stay away from the *cantinas*.

Mexican feelings toward getting drunk also have two extremes. On one hand, to be *borracho* (drunk) is not acceptable; on the other, it is required. You will see little drunkeness on a day-to-day basis, but during a *fiesta* or wedding reception expect it to be the norm. In fact, by not getting drunk at a wedding you may doom the marriage! Also, many Indian rituals require the participants to get drunk. Use your judgement, as you would at home, as to where and how much to drink.

MACHISMO

Machismo (manliness) is a trait that runs throughout Mexico. You will encounter it on the road when a bus driver passes you on a hill or blind curve

Tequila

The native drink of Mexico, tequila, dates back at least to the Aztecs and maybe even earlier. Tequila is made from the hearts of the *agave tequilana weber* (blue agave) plant, and only plants grown in certain areas (primarily Jalisco) are allowed to be utilized in the production of any product called "tequila." A blue agave takes ten or more years to mature. After harvesting the plant, the heart is removed, baked in an earth-covered oven, chopped into small pieces, and ground to extract its juice. This juice is then fermented in ceramic pots and distilled to produce a "no frills" product. Much of the tequila production in Mexico today continues to be done by hand in small distilleries that use the same methods they did hundreds of years ago.

Most tequilas are 51 percent distilled, fermented juice of the blue agave and the rest is either sugar cane juice or other agave extracts. Top quality brands are 100 percent blue agave and will be so noted on the label. All tequilas are approximately 40 percent alcohol; it is the flavor and smoothness that sets them apart. There are four types of tequila: basic "white" (or silver) tequila is the straight, unaged stuff without any additions; "gold" tequila is still unaged, but contains a color-enhancing additive (usually caramel); tequila *reposado* (rested), which has been aged for a short period of time and coloring and flavorings are usually added; and tequila *añejo* (aged) which has been kept in oak barrels for at least a year after distillation, and color and flavoring are usually added. While tequila drinkers outside Mexico are probably familiar with only the major brands (Jose Cuervo and Sauza, to name two), there are many local brands (comparable to estate-bottled wines) that claim to be much superior to the mass-produced variety available outside Mexico.

The traditional way of drinking tequila involves licking a small amount of salt (to raise a protective coating of saliva on the tongue) and taking a straight shot of the liquor, followed by sucking on a lime wedge (which cleanses the tongue of the tequila residues). A *norteamericano* invention, the margarita, made of tequila, lime juice, and Cointreau served in a salt-rimmed glass is considered a "sissy" way of consuming tequila by most Mexicans, as it dilutes the flavor of the liquor. A frozen margarita is considered almost a sin. Whatever way you decide to try this national drink, be careful—it has been the downfall of many a *gringo* or *gringa* who has tried to keep up with the locals! ✪

An encounter with a tour group will give you the opportunity to make new friends.

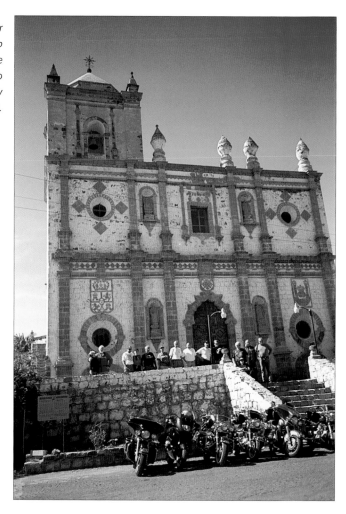

just to prove he has more courage than you. It will come to the forefront at any slight or perceived slight to a man's virility. This might include your showing disbelief regarding a statement that is obviously a complete lie. The best way to avoid trouble is to just mind your own business and be friendly. Let the other guy be the better man.

For women, Mexican *machismo* creates other problems. The typical Mexican man sees his mother, wife, daughters, sisters, and other female relatives as pure, sweet, and to be ever-protected from danger and the real world. They are treated with the utmost courtesy and respect. All other women are basically fair game for this man among men. This is usually reflected by his making a lewd suggestion upon encountering a single woman, although this will be more a show for his friends than an actual invitation. The best way to deal with this behavior is to avoid situations where it may occur. If possible, travel in the company of others, dress conservatively, and carry yourself with dignity. Should you encounter a display of *machismo*, ignore it and continue on your way.

DRESS

Arriving in a small village or even medium-sized city in your riding gear will make you the focus of attention. Often you will be asked about the purpose of it all and your gear may be touched and examined closely. Enjoy the attention and be patient. What you wear when you are not in riding gear is more important, however. Mexicans are very intolerant of any nudity or improper showing of skin. Men are rarely without a shirt except when they are working in the fields or at the beach. Women generally dress from head to toe. A *gringo*, or more importantly, a *gringa* without proper coverage, as deemed by the locals, will invite lewd comments, dismay, and maybe even a warning from the local police to change your attire. Dress conservatively, except at the international resorts. As throughout the world, people in the larger cities are used to seeing stupid tourists dressed in outlandish costumes and tend to be more tolerant.

Realize that the display of the Mexican flag or even its colors on clothing is a no-no. I was once traveling with a friend who had a Mexican flag bandana tied around his neck as we were entering the country. The officials refused to process his paperwork until it was removed. Also, articles of clothing purchased from an Indian are best worn after leaving the area, as there may be meanings in the designs that you do not understand.

SIESTAS

Siesta is one of my most favorite Mexican customs. In Mexico, the main meal of the day is lunch, and this is followed by an afternoon nap—a wonderful custom that originated in Spain. It can cause some difficulty for the traveler, in that most of the shops and stores (including banks) will be closed from 1 p.m. to 4 p.m., reopening again later for several hours. When you are on the road, plan around this custom; when you are having a rest day, enjoy it. However, be warned that *siestas* can become addictive!

BEGGARS AND STREET VENDORS

Mexico is a poor country, but you will be amazed at the ways these ingenious people have discovered to try to make a peso or two. At service stations, children will be trying to clean your windshield with a dirty rag, or

Buy a sack of oranges and make some friends. Then give them away down the road and make more friends.

sell you trinkets or candy. Also, in the larger cities it is common to see Indian women with babies sitting on the sidewalks begging, although I have been told that many of these Indian women are trucked into the cities in the morning by a "manager" and most of their daily take goes to him. Let your conscience be your guide. A few pesos here and there will not inflate the cost of your trip that much and may do some good. Personally, I never give to a beggar, but if someone is offering a service or goods, I might make a small purchase, say of some candies or gum, and then give it to others as I travel down the road. If you do not want what is being offered, a friendly, *"No, gracias,"* with a smile will send them on their way.

PROSTITUTION AND THE "NO-TELL" MOTEL

Prostitution is a legal and accepted practice in most of Mexico. The health hazards of partaking in this activity are the same here as they are all over the world. A Mexican bordello, usually located on the outskirts of town, is considered a place to meet friends, have a few drinks, and pass a pleasant evening. I have been told that many bordellos make most of their profit from customers who just come in to drink and gossip with their friends. Should you wish to visit one of these places, just ask a taxi driver to take you.

Another common feature of most Mexican towns is the "no-tell" motel, usually located on the outskirts of town, surrounded by a high fence. The rooms have individual parking garages with curtains that can be drawn to hide the identity of the vehicle within. Although these are sometimes bordellos, most are commonly used for "meetings" between a Mexican man and his mistress. They can offer a suitable overnight stop for a traveler, as they are clean and quiet and parking is secure. When inquiring about a room, make it very clear that you want the room for the entire night and that is the only service you will need. Because of their purpose, these places usually do not have restaurant facilities.

BARTERING

As a general rule, prices for goods and services in Mexico are subject to negotiation, except in larger department stores and *mercados*. (Be assured that the price you will pay for a Coke on the side of the road will be higher than what the locals pay. However, it is generally not negotiable.) When making any purchase at a market or buying a souvenir, bargaining is an accepted and expected practice. Even at an upscale jewelry store in a tourist destination such as San Miguel de Allende, the price shown on the item won't be the selling price. On smaller purchases, haggling is probably not worth the

The Day of the Dead, on October 31 each year, is a celebration in Mexico when families honor and respect their departed loved ones. Many people actually spend the night in the cemetery.

You can't have a fiesta without balloons.

effort, but on larger ones it can save you up to 50 percent of the original asking price. Enter into and enjoy the give and take of this process; understand up front that the seller will make a profit on any transaction, whatever your level of skill.

FIESTAS

The opportunity for a party or celebration is never overlooked in Mexico. If there is no reason for a *fiesta,* one will be found. *Fiestas* are often distinguished with colorful clothing, children everywhere running and playing, music that reaches higher than normal pitches, and fireworks. In fact, your first indication of a *fiesta* may be your being awakened to the sound of fireworks! Many *fiestas* are associated with church holidays or particular saints' days. Important dates in Mexican history, such as Cinco de Mayo, or even a person's birthday might be celebrated with a *fiesta*. When you encounter a *fiesta,* stop and enjoy the activities. It will certainly add to the richness of your visit.

ASKING FOR DIRECTIONS

Mexicans are eager to please—but this can often lead to trouble and misunderstandings. If you make a request that someone cannot possibly fulfill, you will not get a "no;" instead, you will get a well-intended wrong answer. This becomes particularly troubling when asking for directions. Even when a person has no idea of where you wish to go, he will give it his best shot. Because of this, it may be best to ask several people for directions and hope to get some confirmation by consensus. Also, this can be troubling when requesting a service of someone. Even when they know it cannot possibly be done today or tomorrow, they will tell you that it can be done rather than disappoint you. Be aware of this trait and factor it into all your dealings.

TIME

The idea of being "on time" does not exist in most Mexican environments. Life is to be enjoyed, not rushed. *Mañana* literally means "tomorrow;" in reality, it means "sometime." If a restaurant is to open at 7:00 a.m., that generally means that the staff will show up about that time and begin preparations for serving customers sometime after that. The best way to handle this situation is be prepared for it and relax.

There are many more differences between our cultures. Please take the time to read Carl Franz's *The People's Guide to Mexico* (John Muir Publications) before you go. It will greatly add to the enjoyment of your trip.

A Brief History of Mexico

The following is a very brief outline of Mexican history. It is not intended to be complete, only to give you a feel for the background of the people you will encounter during your ride. Please utilize other sources to fully appreciate the long, wonderful, and often tragic story of Mexico and its people.

It appears that Mexico was originally settled more than 15,000 years ago by people migrating from Asia across the land bridge at the Bering Strait. For many thousands of years, these hunters and wanderers left little sign of their existence. Starting about 3500 B.C.E., however, villages and farms started to appear, and it was these people who formed the bedrock of Mexico's Indian population.

Between 1200 and 500 B.C.E., the **Olmecs** flourished on the Gulf coast and left us with many signs of an advanced civilization, as well as many mysteries that are the subject of much debate among scholars today. The Olmecs were noted for carving massive stone faces with Oriental features. Where did the features on these carvings originate? We do know that the art, religion, and beliefs of the Olmecs had a significant impact on later, better-known cultures. Their civilization perished for unknown reasons, perhaps as the result of war. Today it is believed that the Mayas of the south were direct descendants of the Olmecs.

Another great civilization of northern Mexico was centered in **Teotiuacan,** near modern day Mexico City, and it existed until the 7th century. In 400 C.E., the population of this city was estimated at more than 200,000. These people had a written language and a complicated mathematical system. Again, the reason for the downfall of this civilization is unknown. Perhaps it overgrew its capacity to feed itself or was conquered by aggressors. This site came to have important religious significance to the later Aztecs, who called it the **"Birthplace of the Gods."**

The Aztec era in Mexico began in the first half of the 14th century. These wandering people, led by priests, had been looking for a sign, an eagle perched on a cactus with a snake in its mouth, and they found it near the present-day site of Mexico City. This symbol is on the Mexican flag even today. By the mid-15th century, the **Aztecs** had become the dominant player in the region, forming an alliance with two other powerful tribes to rapidly conquer outlying tribes and districts. Although theirs was a very advanced civilization, the Aztecs believed that human sacrifice to the gods was the only way to gather favors and ensure their continued existence. Their ready domination of others and bloodthirst for tributes ultimately made it easy

Mexicans need little excuse for a fiesta. (courtesy of MotoDiscovery)

for the Spanish to find allies against this awesome nation.

In 1519, a 34-year old Spaniard named **Hernán Cortés** led an unauthorized expedition of approximately 550 men in search of the rumored wealth of Mexico. At this time, the Aztecs controlled an area stretching from the Yucatan Peninsula to the Pacific, with at least 350 individual nations as their subjects. The Spanish landed near present-day Veracruz, but when the men learned of the power of the Aztec many wanted to depart—a problem Cortes overcame by having all the boats burned.

The Spanish had an unforseen advantage, however, in the Aztec legend of the god **Quetzalcoatl,** a wise, kind, fair-skinned, bearded ruler who had sailed east in a boat because of an indiscretion which had disgraced him. Coincidentally, the Aztecs believed he would return specifically in the year 1519 to retake his rightful throne. Since Cortes fit the picture quite well, the Aztecs delayed any actions against the Spanish until they were sure that Cortes was not, indeed, Quetzalcoatl. The Spanish also unwittingly introduced smallpox, malaria, and other European diseases, such as STDs, to the non-resistant native population, with devastating results. By the time the *conquistadors* defeated the Aztecs under their last ruler, **Cuauhtemoc,** the population had been decimated by these diseases. So it came to be that the very small Spanish forces were able to overcome such a powerful nation. Thus began more than 300 years of colonial rule in Mexico.

From their central Mexico base, the Spanish continued their explorations and conquests. The Spanish domination of Mexico was driven by both greed and religious zeal. The land was divided into large *encomiedas,* rights to land and slaves. Many of the padres tried to stop the horrible abuses to which the enslaved natives were subjected, but they were not successful. The discovery of the huge **La Bufa silver mine** at Zacatecas in 1540 further fueled Spanish conquest and the era of exploitation rapidly grew. Exploration and claims for land eventually reached as far north as Colorado. Native Indians were forced to mine the newly found riches and the church gained great power and wealth along with the governing families. The padres who accompanied the *conquistadors* established missions along these routes to convert the "pagan" Indians. By 1605 the Indian population had been reduced from an estimated 25 million at the time of the Spanish landing, to just over one million by disease, murder, and mistreatment.

In this new order, a person's place in society was determined by skin color, birthplace, and parentage. At the top were people who were Spanish-born, known as *peninsulares.* These people obviously represented a very small percentage of the population, but they controlled the country and its wealth. They were considered nobility in Nueva España. Next were the *criollos,* born of Spanish parents in Mexico. This was the class that developed the mining, ran businesses, and very quickly demanded political power. At the bottom of the ladder were the *mestizos* (people of mixed race) and, of course, the native Indians. Although the development of northern Mexico continued at an almost frantic pace for nearly 300 years, unrest and resentment were growing.

On September 16, 1810, **Father Miguel Hidalgo,** a parish priest in Dolores, made his now-famous **Grito de Dolores.** In this call for independence, Hidalgo urged the people to "recover the lands stolen 300 years ago from your forefathers by the hated Spaniards." The town would later be renamed **Dolores Hidalgo** in honor of him, the "Father of the Revolution." The guiding principles of the revolution included the abolition of royal privileges and ownership, the abolition of slavery, and sovereignty for the people. For the next 12 years fighting would continue and many of today's Mexican heroes would emerge, among them **Ignacio Allende** and **Vicente Guerrero.** The revolution was successful in 1821, and in 1824 a constitution was enacted. Mexico's first president, **Guadalupe Victoria,** was sworn into office.

A stable government proved hard to obtain, however. Between 1833 and

The influence of the Catholic Church is seen everywhere in Mexico.

1855, the presidency of Mexico changed hands 33 times. This included 11 terms by **Antonio Lopez de Santa Anna.** He is best known in the U.S. as the general who led his troops at the battle of the **Alamo** in 1836. The dispute over the northern border of Mexico with the U.S. would continue for 11 years and was finally established only after an invasion of the U.S. army, led by **General Winfield Scott.** This "army of occupation" would land at Veracruz in March 1847 and march to the capital. The young military cadets who defended Chapultepec Castle, the last place of resistance in Mexico City, are known as **Los Niños Heroes** and they are remembered every September 13th in a ceremony at their monument in Chapultepec Park.

In 1861, a Zapotec Indian named **Benito Juarez** was elected president. From an orphaned home and abject poverty, he had worked hard and become a lawyer. The story of his accession to this high office against almost overwhelming odds make him one of Mexico's most beloved historical figures. You will find many streets and plazas throughout Mexico bearing his name. Juarez had an ambitious agenda of education reform and established the *rurales,* a rural police force. Although he made many economic reforms,

This statue of Pancho Villa, located in Zacatecas, is only one of many you will find throughout Mexico. (courtesy of MotoDiscovery)

Juarez faced enormous problems with foreign debt and declared a two-year moratorium on their repayment. Millions were owed to France, and **French Emperor Napoleon III** seized the opportunity to add to his empire, invading Veracruz in late 1861.

An early Mexican victory over the French forces at the city of Puebla on May 5, 1862 is now celebrated each year as the **Cinco de Mayo.** Although they never succeeded in completely conquering Mexico, the French were eventually able to take over the central sections of the country, including Mexico City, and Napoleon sent the Austrian archduke, **Maximilian of Hapsburg** to be the emperor of Mexico. Shortly thereafter, however, France began withdrawing troops in response to pressure from the U.S. With the vast majority of his forces returned to Europe, the emperor had no support. The Mexican Army prevailed and defeated the French at **Queretaro** during May of 1867. Maximilian was shot by a firing squad and Juarez was restored to office.

For almost a third of a century, 1876–1910, Mexico was in the hands of a dictator, **Porfirio Diaz.** He quickly developed the country with industry, a railway system, and foreign investment, and the gap between the "haves" and "have-nots" rapidly widened. Large land holdings were established where the common man was basically a slave to the owner. One such holding exceeded seven million acres! As conditions continued to deteriorate for the average Mexican, the country once again became ripe for revolution.

1910 would bring on six years of intense fighting for control of Mexico. Unless you are a scholar of Mexican history, it is truly hard to follow the various and often changing alliances during this period. The names of famous leaders and generals are revered throughout Mexico today. **Francisco Madero, Emiliano Zapata,** and **Pancho Villa** were leaders of various factions during this time. Finally, in 1917 a stable government was established and the constitution that was enacted is still in force today.

Private ownership of land in Mexico became a privilege, not a right, and land seized during the Porfirio years was restored to local communities and the people could work it, not own it. Foreign ownership of land was limited. A minimum wage was established and workers were allowed to form unions. The power of the church was reduced. The reform continued through the presidency of **Lazaro Cardenas** in the 1930s with redistribution of land and nationalization of the foreign-owned oil companies giving birth to PEMEX, the government-owned oil company that exists today.

In 1929 the **Institutional Revolutionary Party (PRI)** was formed and it has maintained control of the Mexican government until the year 2000 when **Vicente Fox,** with a coalition of opposition parties, gained the presidency of Mexico after years of gradually gaining power in the more rural areas of the country. Tales of corruption in the election process abound. Whatever the case, the country has now enjoyed more than eighty years of peace, although economic ups and downs have caused problems with the economy, and scandals and stories of corruption have often caused setbacks. In spite of these misfortunes, northern Mexico now has a good infrastructure and many industrial facilities. The enactment of the North American Free Trade Agreement (NAFTA) in 1990 accelerated this progress tremendously as vast amount of foreign capital flowed in. New factories were built creating many new jobs. These modern facilities coexist with the rich historical sites very well and the government has made great efforts to preserve the heritage.

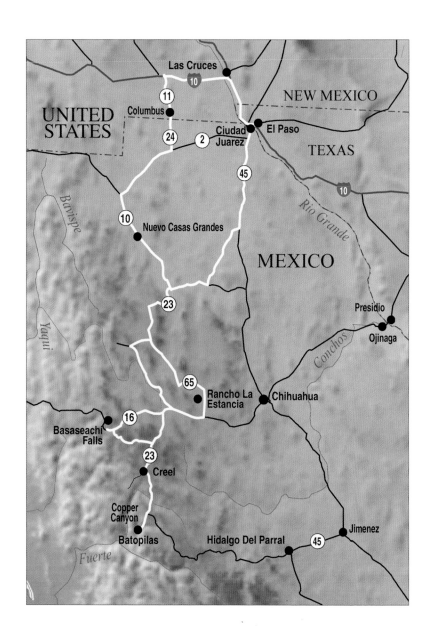

Copper Canyon

Starting and ending in El Paso, this seven-day trip includes approximately 950 miles of riding and a day in and around the Barranaca de Cobre, Mexico's Copper Canyon. The daily mileages are intentionally kept short to allow plenty of time to savor people and sights of this portion of northern Mexico. Copper Canyon, located in one of the most remote areas in Mexico, is a little known series of canyons which truly dwarfs its better known northern neighbor, the Grand Canyon, being more than four times its size and with walls extending 6,000 feet in depth. In addition to this natural beauty you will get some great riding through country populated by descendents of Mormon pioneers who now operate some of the most successful farming operations in Mexico and the shy and elusive Tarahumara Indians.

An excellent road through the mountains makes the ride from Parral to Creel a delight. (photo by Dan Kennedy)

Day 1   El Paso, Texas to Columbus, New Mexico

Distance: *Approximately 145 miles*
Features: *This day of easy riding is designed to let you arrive in El Paso or do some sightseeing (see Wild West Texas chapter above for more information about El Paso) before heading out of town and positioning yourself on the border at Columbus, New Mexico. The border crossing here is much less hectic and easier to traverse than those in El Paso. Also, you should have some time to explore the small town of Columbus, which has the dubious distinction of being the only town in the continental U.S. to ever be invaded by a foreign army.*

Take I-10 West out of El Paso through **Las Cruces, New Mexico** and on to **Deming** (100 miles). The state of New Mexico operates a well-supplied welcome center that can sometimes be helpful in obtaining discount coupons for motel stays as well as supplying brochures and visitor information. At Deming exit onto Hwy. 11 South and after 32 miles of riding through

It can sometimes get lonely when you have a mechanical problem in the desert...where is that master link I meant to pack?

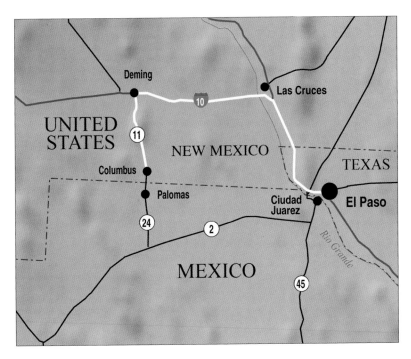

some of the most remote area you have ever ridden you will arrive in Columbus. Please note that Deming will be your last chance to get any last minute repairs or supplies for your bike over the next week. If you are running late, please stop overnight in Deming. I made the mistake of "pushing" on to Columbus late one night and when the lights of that city finally appeared, I swore never to do that again. It got real lonely out there!

Lodging in **Columbus** is difficult. By far the best is **Martha's Place** (www.marthasplacenm.com, 575-531-2467, 5 rooms, $70) located at the corner of Lima and Main. This stucco style building offers clean rooms, a gracious host, and a full breakfast in the mornings. It is strongly suggested that you make reservations for your stay here as the other alternatives are not very attractive. Should you not find a place to your liking, simply backtrack to Deming where suitable accommodations are plentiful. There is excellent camping available at **Pancho Villa State Park** (505-531-2711) at the junction of Hwys. 9 and 11.

In 1916 **Pancho Villa** and his "army" invaded Columbus, New Mexico, killed 24 people, rode off with over 100 horses and mules, and then retreated into Mexico. It is said that this raid was in retaliation for the U.S. government selling him the wrong caliber ammunition for his rifles. This gives Columbus the dubious distinction of being the only city in the

Pancho Villa, the original "outlaw" biker, actually did consider mounting his men on iron horses. (Photo courtesy of the El Paso Public Library)

continental U.S. ever to be invaded by a foreign armed force. **General Pershing** and the U.S. army pursued Villa and his band shortly thereafter into Mexico but were never able to corral him and bring him to justice.

Today Columbus is just another small, dusty border town with a population of just under 2,000. It does its best to take advantage of this historical happening and the state of New Mexico just recently completed a 1.8 million dollar museum with excellent displays and exhibits to commemorate this event at Pancho Villa State Park.

Francisco "Pancho" Villa

So many legends exist regarding the exploits of Pancho Villa that it is difficult to determine fact from fiction. You can be sure, however, that he is still a hero to the poor people of Mexico and any comment by a *gringo* degrading his name or actions will be met with hostility.

Born about 1879 in San Juan del Rio as Doroteo Arango, little is known of Villa's early years, but he was of the peasant class and life must have been hard indeed. At the age of 16, he killed a man in Durango for allegedly molesting one of his sisters. From this time on he lived a life of crime, and by the age of 20 he had added cattle stealing and bank robbery to the list of crimes for which he was wanted. From 1900 until 1910, he and his gang lived in the Sierra Madre Occidental and established a Robin Hood reputation with the locals, robbing and stealing at will, while always escaping the efforts of government troops *(rurales)* to capture them.

In 1910, Mexico's presidential election pitted the ruling capitalist party against the growing opposition of various groups looking for socialist reforms and help for the lower classes. The election was corrupt and revolution filled the air. Villa took this opportunity to come down from the mountains and join with other groups to form the Division del Norte. In this way, he transformed himself and his followers from *banditos* to *revolucionarios.*

Although Villa successfully liberated the states of Sonora and Chihuahua, he was not able to maintain a strong central government. It wasn't until 1916 that peace and order returned to the country, and that was only accomplished by the intervention of the U.S. government.

In 1919, Villa retired to Canutillo with his comrades, known as *dorados* (the golden ones). On July 20, 1923, while on a banking trip into Parral, seven riflemen pumped more than 150 bullets into his Dodge automobile. It has been rumored that they were hired by the government because Villa was too popular with the people. Over 30,000 people attended his funeral.

Even in death, Villa would cause controversy. Three years after he was buried in Parral, someone dug up the body and cut off the head, and it has never been found. Three years after this incident, the federal government ordered the body to be moved to a special tomb in Mexico City for heroes of the revolution. Local legend has it that the body was switched with one from an adjoining grave and the body now in Mexico City is not Villa's. ✪

Day 2 Columbus to Nuevo Casas Grandes

Distance *Approximately 130 miles*
Features *An easy border crossing, introduction to Mexican roads and traffic habits, a ride into the interior with a wonderful overnight destination that has lots of interesting things to do and people to meet.*

The border crossing here at **Palomas** has much less traffic than the more crowded and hectic ones in El Paso. As you cross the border make an immediate right into the gravel parking lot, take your necessary documents (see entrance requirements) into the customs and immigration building and you should be on your way in a very short time. Even though this is a 24-hour crossing point, do not expect all services (i.e. copiers, etc.) to be available outside normal business hours or on Sundays or holidays (come prepared or be prepared to be delayed). It is strongly suggested that you take just a minute or two before remounting your steed and continuing on to examine all your papers and the decal on your bike to make sure everything is

Be careful—these guys are not always tethered.

in proper order. Now is the time and place to correct any mistakes or "glitches." You don't want to travel 90 miles into Mexico before realizing that backtracking is necessary to change one small numerical error.

Exit the parking lot to the right and continue through town on Hwy. 24 for approximately 18 miles (32 km) to the T-intersection with Hwy. 2. Don't be confused by some "official" looking buildings or signs along this stretch. At this T-intersection, turn right and follow Hwy. 2 for approximately 70 miles (113 km) to the intersection with Hwy. 10 on the outskirts of **Jamos** where you will turn left toward **Nuevo Casas Grandes**. Your paperwork will be checked shortly after making this turn.

Up until this point you will be riding good high-speed, two-lane road, with lots of truck traffic. Relax and enjoy the desert scenery, getting anxious now and passing marginally will save you very little time; the day is short and better roads and riding lie ahead! After clearing the customs check, which will be on your right, just a mile or two after the turn the traffic disappears and you can have a delightful ride through the desert for the next 30 miles (54 km) to your destination for the evening.

On a hot day in the desert highlands, shade will be where you find it.

Nuevo Casas Grandes, a modern city with a population of 80,000 or so, is a center of agriculture and trading, and provides services for the tourists who come to visit the nearby **Paquime Indian ruins** (see sidebar). In the late 1800s, Mormons fleeing the polygamy laws in the U.S. settled near here. The modern farming techniques they introduced here have had dramatic results, and growing fruit and making cheese are the main industries in the area. They even have their own packing company to ship their product to the U.S. and throughout Mexico.

For an interesting side trip, visit the Mormon settlement of **Colonia Juarez,** approximately 18 mi. (30 km) southwest of Nuevo Casas Grandes via Hwy. 18. These people are proud of their heritage and accomplishments and are more than willing to enlighten you as to the history and background of the area. Colonia Juarez has a bilingual school for grades one through twelve that provides graduates with certificates accepted both in Mexico and the U.S. Over 80 percent of its graduates continue on to college.

Nuevo Casas Grandes is prosperous and reminds me more of a southwestern U.S. town than of Mexico, but it is a good first night's stop, as all the necessary services will be available and there are some interesting side trips nearby. There is a bypass, but you will want to stay on the main highway marked CENTRO, which will put you on a wide avenue that runs

The Paquime Ruins

The Paquime ruins represent all that remain of a civilization that existed for 700 years. The first people to practice agriculture in northwest Mexico, they were known to have been in existence as early as 700 C.E., and the influence of the Paquime probably peaked during the 12th century. Located on the banks of the river, their multi-story adobe city was the focal point of trading during the 11th and 12th centuries for the American southwest and southern Mexico. The size of these buildings are the origin of the town's name, Casas Grandes (big houses). The city was abandoned in the mid-1300s, possibly due to destruction by enemies from the north, and fire. Whatever the reason, the people left the city and where they went remains a mystery.

These complex structures not only had running water brought from springs to the north, but also a water refuse system to remove wastes. The multi-roomed, multi-storied buildings were fitted together in a jumble of angles and the rooms may have up to sixteen interior walls each. It appears these rooms were heated and many had exterior windows for ventilation. The doorways are of a T-shape that allow only one person at a time to pass, while still allowing for items to be carried through in the arms. It is believed this was done for defensive purposes. The excavated portions of the town include ball courts, military encampments, a platform for making offerings to the gods, and ceremonial plazas. A stone cross lying on the ground with its arms aligned with the points of the compass appears to have been used to predict the seasons.

To reach the Paquime ruins from Nuevos Casas Grandes, continue south, making a right turn toward Casas Grandes, and watch for a sign indicating the left turn to the ruins (approx. 6 miles or 10 km).   ✪

through the center of town. In my opinion, the best hotel in town is the **Motel Hacienda** on the main drag, (2603 Avenue Juarez, 011-52-169-1046, $65). The rooms are clean and spacious, the staff is friendly and mostly bilingual, and the restaurant is more than adequate serving a great hot breakfast in the mornings. It has a pool surrounded by a nice courtyard. If you ask for a room on the courtyard, you can park your bike by your door. There are many other accommodations in this city, some of which are of equal value. Most are located on Ave. Juarez.

Day 3   Nuevo Casas Grandes to Creel

Distance   *255 miles (410 km)*
Features   *This is a straightforward, good road, running mostly through high desert leading into high pine forest, before winding through the Sierra Madre Occidental and arriving in Creel.*

Follow Hwy. 10 south from Nuevo Casas Grandes for approximately 50 miles (80 km) to the intersection with Hwy. 23 in **Buenaventura.** Turn right on Hwy. 23 toward Gómez Farias. After about 42 miles (71 km) turn right at the PEMEX station toward Madera and **Cuidad Guerrero.** There is a fairly good restaurant on the right after the turn, as well as a small grocery store. After about 7 miles (11 km) turn left toward Cuidad Guerrero which you will reach in 60 miles (98 km). Another 12 miles (20 km) will bring you to **La Junta** where you will turn right and then another left towards **Creel** which you will reach in 60 miles (98 km).

Need a little dual-sport time? (Photo by Dan Kennedy)

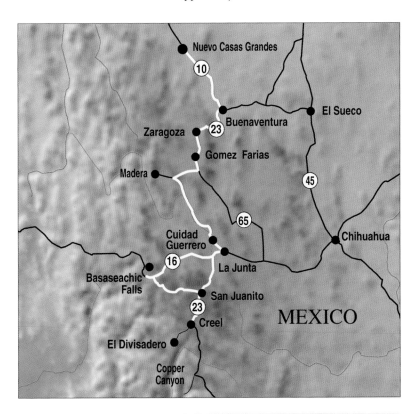

Side Trip

About 12 miles (20 km) beyond La Junta Hwy. 23 separates from Hwy. 16 with a left turn toward Creel. If you were to continue straight on Hwy. 16 for approximately 50 miles (80 km), you'd be at **Casada de Basaseachic** (Basaseachic Falls), the third highest waterfall in North America at 1,000 feet. The park itself is pristine, with at least five other waterfalls, but outside the park, logging and overgrazing have eroded the natural beauty of the area. To view the falls, plan on a one-hour, round-trip walk to and from the viewpoint. If you wish to go down to the bottom of the falls, plan on a three-hour hike (two hours uphill). If you take this side trip, add an additional four hours to your day. After visiting the falls, retrace your route for only a short way and take the right turn marked to San Juanito (Creel) and then after turning right at the T-intersection approximately 58 miles (97 km) later, continue on to Creel as above.

Placed in a valley at approximately 7,700 ft. in altitude and consisting of about 3,000 souls, **Creel** is primarily a logging town that is slowly turning into a tourist stop, as it is acknowledged as the jumping-off point for visiting the **Copper Canyon**. All services will be available in Creel: gasoline, hotels, laundry, restaurants, souvenir shops, and whatever else you might need. Although the town has a frontier feeling, overlooking the city from a nearby hill is a statue of Christ blessing the whole goings-on.

The **Motel Parador de la Montaña** (45-600-23, $65, 41 Ave. Lopez Mateos) is your basic 1950s motel that has a comfortable feeling about it with Mexican ambiance. The rooms are more than adequate and have all amenities. However, there are many alternatives. Should you wish to really splurge, continue on to El Divisadero (5 miles) to the **Hotel Divisadero Barrancas** *(Sandy's Choice)* which has 52 beautifully appointed rooms, many with balconies, literally hanging over and looking into the Copper Canyon. It is rather pricy at $180/night during the months of June, July, and August and $220/night the rest of the year. These prices do include

Tarahumara Indians

The actual name for these very secretive and quiet people is the Raramuri, which means "running people;" the name "Tarahumara" is the result of a corruption by the invading Spanish.

When the Spanish expanded into the area of central Chihuahua, the Tarahumara occupied the more fertile lands. As attempts to "civilize," enslave, or baptize them became more intense, they moved further into the rugged highlands of the Sierra Madre Occidental, a migration which continues even to this day. They are a people committed to continuing their own way of life, language, customs, and religion, even at the expense of modern-day comforts. Although they have been studied by many eminent scholars, no one has really ever been able to invade the culture and thinking of these people.

In Creel and Batopilas you will encounter Tarahumara selling their wares on the streets. They are extremely shy and won't look you in the eye. They do not live in these towns, but are semi-nomadic, living outside the towns in caves or stone huts and moving up and down the mountains according to the season. Do not ever presume to enter a Tarahumara home or take a photograph without first obtaining permission.

These "running people" have the amazing ability to run for days kicking a small wooden ball with their feet, covering 40–60 miles a day, depending on the terrain. It is also said that they can capture deer and other animals by running them to the point of exhaustion. In 1968 the Mexican government entered two Tarahumara in the 26-mile Olympic marathon, but they did not finish at the top. They maintained that the "shortness" of the race and the fact that they were forced to wear shoes made it not worth the effort. Perhaps we should introduce a 60-mile, barefoot marathon.

To me, the most amazing thing about the Tarahumara has been their ability to maintain their culture through centuries of constant conflict. When you encounter these people, please respect their 400-year old commitment to maintain their privacy. ✪

three meals each day. It has been my experience, however, that if you show up late in the day and are willing to do your meals a la carte, the price is very flexible. This hotel does not have phone service but reservations can be made through a central booking office (888-232-4219).

Day 4 and 5   Exploring Copper Canyon

Distance *Your total distance will be approximately 160 miles (260 km), including a steep, 24 miles (40 km) dirt grade into and out of the Copper Canyon.*

Features *The goal for the next two days is to see and explore this wonder of nature. I recommend an overnight stop in Batopilas.*

The best way to travel down to the bottom of the canyon is by dual-sport bike. The ride is doable on almost any bike; I have done it on a VFR several times. From Creel, take Hwy. 23 south for about 42 miles (70 km) to the clearly-marked right turn to **Batopilas.** It is a wonderful high mountain road with sweepers, twisties, and a very good surface. Even if you don't intend to descend into the canyon itself, the ride to here and return to Creel is highly recommended.

There is a small grocery store at the turn-off for any last-minute supplies. It is hard to go wrong from here, as there is only one other road off to the

The abundant views from the rim of the Copper Canyon will have you stopping often.
(photo by Dan Kennedy)

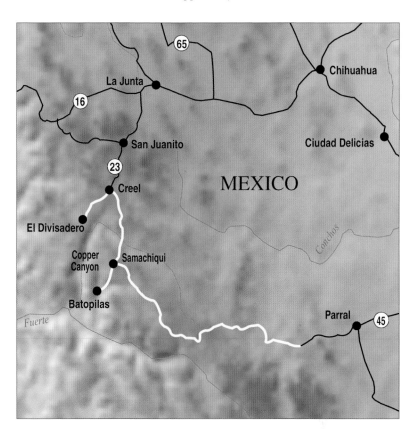

right. After the turn the first 18 miles (30 km) or so is a hard-packed, mostly-level road meandering through the forest. Then the road begins the more than 6,000-foot descent into the canyon. This is not a technically difficult drive—buses and supply trucks make the trip every day—but it is rocky and steep at points and will require your attention. The road has been improved greatly over the past several years and, with the exception of periods after heavy rains, is very doable on almost any bike other than a heavy dresser. The views of the canyon will blow your mind; frequent photo stops are required. Please remember if the sun is wrong for a shot, you will be coming back the next day, as this is the only road in and out. After approximately 24 miles (40 km) you will level off and cross the river bridge into Batopilas.

Batopilas, a town of approximately 600 people, rests in an oasis at the bottom of Copper Canyon. It has a rich history as a mining town. When the Spanish arrived in Batopilas in 1634, they found pure silver rocks weighing up to 500 pounds along the banks of the river. At one time,

Magnificent views and curving, descending dirt roads make for an exciting ride into the Copper Canyon.

As you reach the bottom of the Copper Canyon, you will find the river that exposed vast lodes of silver.

Batopilas was one of the wealthiest towns in Mexico. In fact, it was the second town in Mexico to get electricity.

Eventually, the difficulty in getting ore out of the canyon and the expulsion of the Spanish in the 1820s brought a halt to the mining. However, it was resumed in the mid-1800s (see sidebar). Some gold and silver is still extracted by local independent miners, but the primary industry today is growing marijuana, as evidenced by the disproportionate number of high-priced SUVs parked on the streets next to the mules and horses. Batopilas is by no means a lawless or dangerous town. The locals mind their own business and a casual visitor will not be bothered by or even aware of the goings-on. If you ride your bike into Batopilas, however, expect to be inspected for drugs both going in and coming out.

Most of the buildings in Batopilas date from the mid-to-late 1800s and the town really has a flavor that should not be missed. I would suggest that you take some minimal food with you, as the restaurants and grocery stores seem to work on a schedule of their own. The **Hotel Mary** is the place to stay, and reservations can be made by calling a central booking agent (tel. 15-54-08 or 10-45-80, $30); the hotel itself has no phone. Be sure to request a room with a bath. The rooms surround a very nice courtyard.

The "lost mission" of Batopilas.

The ruins of Shepherd's home and foundry in Batopilas lead one to contemplate the rewards of this world.

Several other facilities exist in town, primarily as guest rooms in private houses. The **Copper Canyon Riverside Lodge,** a restored *hacienda,* is the premier facility in town, but they require a minimum of seven nights' stay in conjunction with tours to other commonly-owned hotels. It is worth strolling in and wandering around, however.

In or nearby Batopilas are several other sights worth a visit:

Lost Cathedral: This mission church is located approximately 4 mi. (7 km) south of town on the only road out, a good dirt road that can be easily handled by a dual-sport bike. Tour operators will surely include it as part of your itinerary. Alternately, you could hire a local truck to take you there and

Batopilas Mining Company

A great deal of what you see in Batopilas today is the result of one man, **Alexander Shepherd,** and his company, the Batopilas Mining Company. Unlike the absent owner who takes treasure out of an area and leaves nothing in return, Shepherd left behind a wonderful legacy.

Batopilas was a great source of silver for the Spanish, but when they were expelled in 1820 the mining stopped. Mexican companies resumed a small amount of mining in the 1840s, but their success was limited. Then an American, John Robinson, bought up some properties thought to be mined out in the early 1860s and discovered *La Veta Grande* (the Great Vein), a hereto unknown source. Robinson either did not realize the size of his discovery, or felt the cost of transporting ore to Chihuahua for processing was prohibitive, because he sold his holdings in Batopilas to another American, Alexander Shepherd, for the goodly sum of $600,000 in 1880.

Shepherd, whose tenure as governor of Washington, D.C., ended when Congress removed him from office for alleged corruption, moved to Batopilas, started buying up other outlying claims, and formed the Batopilas Mining Company. He solved the problem of transporting the ore by building his own refinery and foundry in his Hacienda San Miguel and instead, transported out refined, pure silver ingots. Often the monthly mule train would carry out up to 200 of these ingots, each weighing 70 pounds. Needless to say, Batopilas was one of the wealthiest spots in Mexico.

Shepherd and the wealth created by the Batopilas Mining Company created an incredible city in this remote canyon. Most of the fine homes still standing today were built during its heyday. Theater and the arts blossomed. The company built a viaduct and hydroelectric facility, only the second such in Mexico at the time; it is still the source of the town's electricity today. At its peak, the Batopilas Mining Company was one of the wealthiest companies in the world, paying over $1,000,000 in dividends per year.

Shepherd died in 1902 and the mines played out in the early 1920s, when Batopilas went into decline and the company fell into oblivion—but, the city remains a jewel even today.   ✪

With cliffs towering on either side, the road snakes through the trees at the base of the canyon.

back, or you could (gasp) walk. The date of its founding and the early history of this church are a mystery. The bells have striking dates dating back to 1630, but there is no mention of this church in Vatican records. If the church was founded by Jesuits, later Franciscans may have destroyed their records. In any case, the local people have taken great pride in restoring this church to its former glory.

Hacienda San Miguel: This is the former home and factory of Alexander Shepherd, the founder of the Batopilas Mining Company (see sidebar). The house, foundry, and associated facilities lie in ruins today, overgrown by the lush vegetation that proliferates in the area. It's a short walk to the ruins on the east side of the river.

Aqueduct and power generating plant: In the late 1800s, Shepherd not only built an aqueduct to provide water to the town, he also established a power generating plant. Although it has since been refurbished, this still provides the power source for the town. It is well worth the walk to the north of town, below the bridge, to see this engineering marvel still functioning.

After your visit to Batopilas, retrace your route back to Creel. And enjoy the ride!

An alternate way to get to Batopilas is to make arrangements at your hotel to hire a four-wheel drive vehicle with seats attached on the top to take you into the canyon. This is usually a two-day excursion with overnight in an adequate hotel in Batopilas itself. The cost of this tour can be lessened, of course, if you can find some other brave soul(s) to share. I must say that I have never visited Batopilas by this method and admire those who have. I'm sure they have had the adventure of a lifetime! Me, I'll ride my bike.

Other rides out of Creel are on the new mountain roads to **Parral** and back for 40 or 50 miles, and the trip to **El Divisadero** for a super view of the canyon.

An alternate method of exploring the Copper Canyon is by 4WD van. The couple riding on the roof may lose their fillings by the end of the day, however.

Day 6 Creel to Rancho la Estancia

Distance *120 miles (200 km)*

Features *After the thrills and rigors of the trip into and out of the canyon, this will give you a chance to sleep in and have a short day of good, paved road descending from the heights of Creel into lower flatlands. You'll go through some amazing Mennonite farming country to a wonderful, isolated hunting resort that is truly at "the end of the road."*

Retrace your route up Hwy. 23 north out of Creel 60 miles (98 km) to the T-intersection with Hwy. 16 and take a right turn. At the next T-intersection (the one with the PEMEX station), turn right to continue on Hwy. 16 toward **Cuauhtemoc.** After riding approximately 100 miles (170 km) from Creel, as you are approaching Cuauhtemoc, take a left onto Hwy. 65 toward **Gomez Farias** (just past another PEMEX station). After approximately 12 miles (20 km), you'll see the well-marked dirt road on the left that leads to the **Rancho la Estancia.**

The beautiful Posada Barrancas Mirador offers spectacular views of the canyon and there are fireplaces in every room. The two-hundred dollar a night tariff includes three meals. Views aren't cheap.

This is **Mennonite** country. The *campos menonitas* that are on either side of this ride are numbered instead of named, and each usually consists of 20 or so families. These people maintain a simple lifestyle that reflects their religious beliefs. Do not expect to see anything open in the *campos* on Sunday. The Mennonites believe in no allegiance, except to God. In the 1920s, they asked the government of Mexico for permission to immigrate, but they would not accept military service and wanted to establish their own schools without any swearing of allegiance to the nation. The government wisely agreed, and the Mennonites introduced modern farming techniques that have benefitted all of Mexico to this day. Their first language is a German dialect and you will see business signs in German. The region is known for its *queso menonita* (Mennonite cheese), and a short visit to a *quesería* is a pleasure. Their white cheddar is said to be the best made in Mexico.

The last time I was there, the road to the Rancho was five miles or so of hard-packed dirt. If you have any doubts about traversing the road, stop at the gray house with the stone fence at the turn-off. This is the home of **Mr. Jacobo Dick,** a local Mennonite farmer who will let you park your bike in

Whenever a train is due to arrive at the Copper Canyon, you can be sure that the locals will be there trying to sell their wares. (courtesy of Mexico's Ministry of Tourism)

Tarahumara selling their hand-made wares in El Divisadero.

At a rest stop in the Mennonite farmland between Chihuahua and Creel, riders pause to smell the delicious air and observe cowboys tending their farm. (photo by Dan Kennedy)

his very safe yard and drive you down to the Rancho. (You should offer to pay for this service, but he will probably not accept it.) The Rancho will give you a ride back the next morning.

Hotel Rancho la Estancia (tel. 14-16-16-57, $30) has a 4,000-foot paved landing strip that allows the rich and famous to fly into this isolated area to hunt, drink, and relax away from the prying eyes of the world. It was said to have been a favorite of **Bing Crosby** as well as the **"Rat Pack."** Most of its guests today are Europeans who come for the good hunting. You may very well find yourself as the only English speaking guests! While the accommodations are somewhat basic, they do include two swimming pools, a bar, and good restaurant. This is topped off by a very friendly owner and staff. It is located in a small valley with beautiful, neatly groomed grounds overflowing with flower gardens. Plan to arrive early in the day and enjoy this oasis to its fullest.

Day 7 Rancho la Estancia to El Paso

Distance *Approximately 290 miles (180 km)*
Features *This is a straight forward day of high speed riding. Almost all your day will be on improved four-lane road and toll roads. Please don't let this lull you into a false sense of security. You are still in a foreign country, different laws and customs still apply. I can assure you that you will be experiencing "border fever" however great and enjoyable your trip has been up until now. Relax; stay alert and get ready for the busy border crossing back into the U.S. Be sure and check out with Mexican customs (see entrance requirements).*

Retrace your steps out of the Rancho back to the pavement where you will turn left. After approximately 87 miles (140 km) turn right in the town of **Bavicora** toward **Gómez Farias**, continue on this road to **Buenaventura** 43 miles (71 km) and take a right turn direction **Ricardo Flores Magon** and **Villa Ahumada.** In Ricardo Flores Magon 33 miles (55 km) follow signs to Villa Ahumada and after an additional 56 miles (90 km) you will hook up

This remote hacienda, which dates back to the 1500s, now provides a wonderful overnight stop.

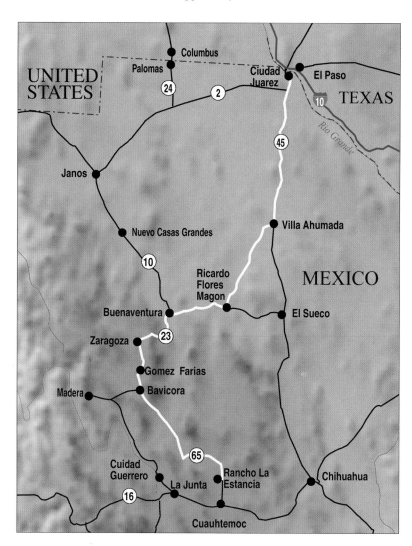

in that town onto the major four-lane Hwy. 45 by making a left in the direction of Ciudad Juarez and El Paso which are now only 68 miles (110 km) away. This is some remote high desert riding at its best. Watch your speed!

As you approach **Ciudad Juarez** just follow the clearly marked signs to the United States. It is your every right to split lanes to the front of the line when traffic backs up at the border crossing but you should be aware that not everyone else is aware of this fact. Use your own judgment. Be prepared to listen to some horn honking, loud words, and witnessing some international hand signals should you choose to exercise these "rights."

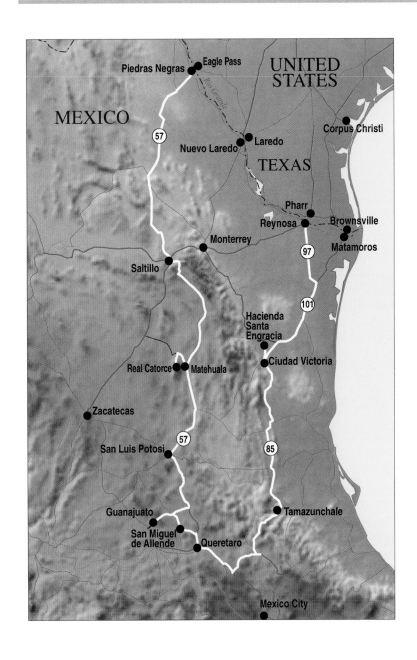

The Colonial Heartland

This route is for those who wish to visit some of the great colonial cities of the Spanish era and experience the glories of traveling through jungles on a portion of the "old" route to and from the U.S. to Mexico City (the Pan American Highway). It truly travels through the heart and soul of Mexico, from the days of the Spanish occupation to the time of revolution. Today it retains much of this history and culture while being one of the most progressive areas in modern Mexico.

The second half of this route puts you into the jungles of eastern Mexico as you twist and turn from more than 6,000 feet in altitude to near sea level. One city on this route is almost deserted with a population that once exceeded 40,000 now reduced to less than 700. Others have continued to grow and are now major metropolitan areas, but still retain the architecture and feel of days of old. The national monument city of San Miguel de Allende is unique in all of Mexico with its colonial architecture, and eclectic mix of people ranging from local Indians to international permanent residents and visitors to local language and art schools.

The riding on this route has something for everyone: long straight desert stretches with mountains in the distance mixed with cobblestone roads dating back to the 1500s to those twisties and curves reminiscent of 1950s mountain travel. The scenery is dramatic. This area also includes the birthplace of the Mexican Revolution and is rich in history. The route is approximately 1,400 miles and outlines seven days of riding. If at all possible plan on a few more days to relax and enjoy.

Day 1 Eagle Pass, Texas, to Saltillo

Distance *260 miles (420 km)*
Features *This day allows for a fairly easy border crossing and high-speed riding through the desert of Northern Mexico. It ends in the modern mountain city of Saltillo with a gem of the old contained within its center.*

The high desert has many strange and wonderful types of growths.

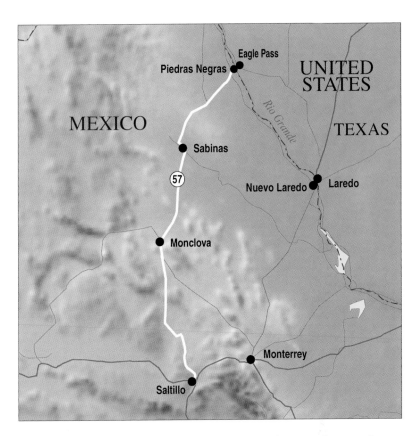

Eagle Pass, Texas, is a small border city of 21,000 that provides a good overnight stop with all the services you might need prior to entering Mexico and an easy and non-crowded border crossing experience. It is located approximately 150 miles southwest of **San Antonio** and 124 miles northwest of **Laredo.**

Eagle Pass grew up around **Fort Duncan** which was established in 1849 as the first fort on the Rio Grande River to protect the area from roaming Indians and Mexican bandits. Some of the original buildings are still standing. Lodging is not a problem here with seemingly all the national chains represented. If you want to try a "local" we recommend the **Eagle Pass Inn,** Main and Bibb (www.eaglepassinn.com, 830-773-1999, $60).

From Eagle Pass follow highway 57 south signs to reach the border town of **Piedras Negras.** This is an unusual crossing in that you get the papers for your person at the border, but do not get the papers for the bike until traveling 36 miles further south. To get through **Piedras Negras** simply follow the Holiday Inn signs until you pick up the signs for Hwy. 57 toward **Saltillo.**

A boy soon learns who his true friends are. (courtesy of Mexico's Ministry of Tourism)

After 36 miles (60 km) you must stop and clear the motorcycle and will probably experience another baggage check. Then follow **Sabinas** and **Monclova** signs until picking up Saltillo signs again. All are clearly marked highway 57. As you enter Saltillo on highway 57, take the bypass marked **Matehuala** or **San Luis Potosi.**

The most comfortable stop for this evening is the **Camino Real Hotel** *(Sandy's Choice)* right on highway 57 as you bypass the city, (844-438-0000, $130). This is a "five star" motel with all amenities you would expect including an outdoor heated pool. The restaurant is excellent as are the views of the valley below from the beautifully landscaped grounds. Should you wish to stay downtown (see below) just follow the centro signs to the **Hotel Colonial Amenda** (www.hotelcolonialamenda.com, 410-00-88, $65) located at Orbgeón 222 just a couple of blocks from the central plaza. This is a comfortable hotel, but secure parking will be a few extra pesos.

A major city with a population approaching one million, **Saltillo** is a major manufacturing center for northern Mexico, producing automobiles, automobile parts, petrochemicals, textiles, and tiles. It is also a major transshipment point for the livestock and farm products grown in the area. Thankfully, this modern industrial complex is situated on the outskirts of town, while the downtown area continues to show its colonial past.

Saltillo was founded in 1577 by the Spanish and soon grew into a major transhipment point on the **Camino Real,** at one time supplying the colonies to the north between Texas and present-day Colorado. It sits in an arid, high mountain valley at more than 5,000 feet, and it is surrounded by the mountains of the **Sierra Madre Oriental.**

The *plaza de armas* is rather barren of local color, but it does contain the **Catedral de Santiago de Saltillo** which is one of the northernmost examples of Spanish church architecture of the late 1700s. You can get a good view of the city from the tower. While the exterior has a magnificent ornate facade, the interior is equally impressive. When lit at night, the *catedral* is truly an impressive sight. The *plaza acuña,* located two blocks north on Calle Allende will give you a much better feel for the town. This shaded square is usually filled in the evenings with families, food vendors, and strolling musicians, and it is surrounded by shops and cafes. The **Mercado Juarez** located on this square is a pleasant place to visit and shop for local handicrafts. If you are a bird lover, the **Museo de las Aves,** located between Allende and Hidalgo just south of the *plaza de armas,* offers wonderful exhibits on nearly 700 species of Mexican birds stuffed and mounted in natural surroundings.

A stop at a Mexican "convenience store" makes for a nice break.

Day 2 Saltillo to Real Catorce

Distance *190 miles (312 km)*
Features *The quest today is to reach the wonderful town of Real Catorce, a magnificent, nearly abandoned mining city.*

It is only 150 miles (240 km) of high speed riding on Hwy. 57 from Saltillo to the right turn to **Real Catorce** about 3 miles (5 km) north of Matehuala onto Hwy. 62 with signs indicating Real Catorce. The first 18 miles (30 km) will be a good, two-lane paved road. As you enter the small town of **Cedral,** just past the PEMEX, a sign indicates a 90-degree left turn. Continue straight at this sign to bypass this small town. A private sign indicating *LIBRAMIENTO A REAL DE CATORCE* was in existence at this turn the last time I was through there.

At the km 28 milepost, the left turn onto the 15 miles (25 km) cobblestone road to Real Catorce will be clearly marked. This road was built in the 1700s to haul out ore, later processed silver, and eventually coins from the mint. The heavily-laden cargo carriers left some deep ruts that still exist today. If you are riding a dual-sport bike, it is an absolute delight, as it climbs through abandoned mines and villages with dramatic vistas to the landscape below. In my opinion, it is passable on a street bike with a rider of

Travel through this tunnel is an adventure unto itself—take care.

reasonable experience, but it will be slow going, especially on a large bike. Please let your own experience be your guide when deciding whether or not to travel this road.

As you approach the town, a real adventure awaits: a one-lane tunnel that was originally a mineshaft. The last vehicle going in is given a red stick which he surrenders when he exits, to signal that it is clear to proceed in the other direction. The directors at each end of the tunnel are also in radio contact—but the system is far from perfect! When you get the O.K. to proceed, be alert for people, burros, and maybe even an oncoming bus. If you see headlights (the tunnel is unlit), look for a wide place or a dug-out place immediately and get over until the oncoming traffic has passed.

As you exit the tunnel there will be good, flat parking on the left. If you are on a street bike, park here and explore the city on foot. A dual-sport can continue on with no difficulty. You will be greeted by several young men who will offer to guide you through the town and a street full of vendors selling local wares. The **Hotel El Real** (887-50-58, $45) located just up the

Parking on the sidewalk outside the Hotel Real is free to all that are brave enough to try it.

It is hard to make a living in a mostly deserted city, but the Hotel Real Catorce does a good job of it.

hill near the church at Morelos 20, is a wonderful place that is full of ambiance and has a good restaurant serving, of all things, good, home cooked Italian food. Secure parking is available nearby at no extra charge. It is an almost mystic experience to stand on the terrace and watch the sunset over this city with abandoned housing for over 40,000 people.

Should you not wish to attempt the cobblestone, the nice, clean, and comfortable **Hotel Las Palmas** (tel. 488- 2-00-01, $50), is located on Hwy. 57 on the left just past the right turn off indicated above on the northern outskirts of **Matehuala**. The hotel is right out of the 1950s with separate accommodations and secure carport parking at your room. It also has a very good restaurant. The staff of the Las Palmas can arrange a car and driver to take you to Real Catorce; the price is negotiable depending on the number of passengers and how long you wish to spend. Matehuala itself, a town of approximately 60,000, is a quiet city with few sights to interest the casual visitor. However, spend an evening sitting around the Plaza Principal and you gain insight as to modern rural Mexican life.

The origin and founding of **Real Catorce** is unclear. It was officially established in 1779, although records of mining activity in the area date back several years before that. During the 1800s, the rich veins at this 9,000-foot altitude produced vast quantities of silver. So much so, in fact, that a mint was built in the city, and this building still exists, located at the **Jardin Hidalgo.** In the late 1800s, a population in excess of 40,000 enjoyed municipal water, electricity, paved streets, a bullring, and other modern conveniences in this remote location. By 1900, the richer veins had been depleted and a slow decline began. The revolution of 1910 stopped commercial mining activity completely. Today, a few hardy individuals continue to eke out a subsistence by mining the remaining areas.

The local church, **Parroquia de la Purisima Concepcion,** contains the **St. Francis** shrine. Devotees believe the image in the shrine has the ability to answer prayers and to cleanse believers of sins. Tens of thousands of believers make a pilgrimage to the shrine during the week of October 4th—the only time of the year you won't find the city almost deserted. The area around Real Catorce is also sacred to the **Huicholes,** who give special significance to the hallucinogenic cactus known as *peyote,* which grows in this area. They visit this area in the spring to collect the *peyote* and perform various religious rituals. Because of these pilgrimages, many believe Real Catorce to be one of the "power points" on earth. It certainly has an atmosphere all to itself.

Day 3 Real Catorce to San Miguel de Allende

Distance *235 miles (379 km)*
Features *This day offers quite a mix from the cobblestone roadway leaving Real Catorce, to high speed rural desert roads and a modern four lane divided highway. Traveling from mountains to open desert plains back to mountains, the day ends at San Miguel de Allende, one of the most visited and beloved of all colonial Mexican cities.*

An uneducated Indian, inspired by a picture on a postcard, oversaw the building of the facade of this church in San Miguel de Allende (courtesy of MotoDiscovery)

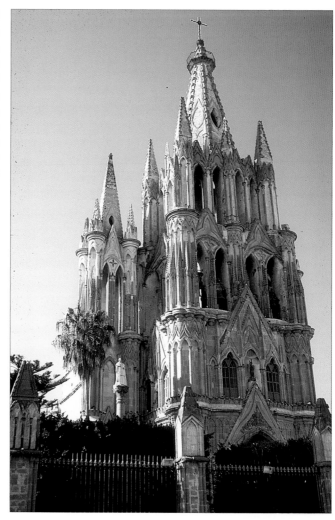

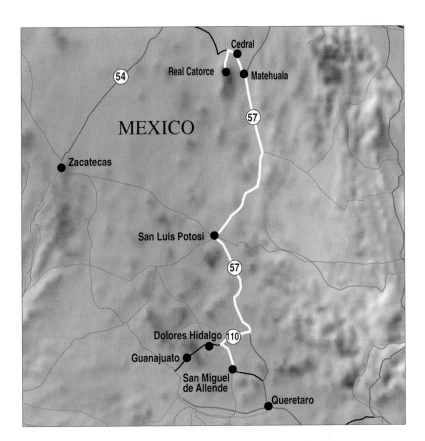

Retrace your route of yesterday out of **Real Catorce** back to Hwy. 57 where you turn right to continue south. Take the clearly marked bypass around **Matehuala** and continue on Hwy. 57. After 85 miles (140 km) you will be approaching **San Luis Potosi**. Take the bypass around this bustling city to save time and avoid the hassle of traffic, and follow the signs to **Querétaro**. About 70 miles (115 km) after rejoining Hwy. 57 south you need to be alert to a right turn onto Hwy. 110 to **Dolores Hidalgo**. Where the road splits after about 20 miles (35 km) turn left and go the final 20 miles (35 km) into **San Miguel de Allende**. Straight ahead on the center square *(El Jardin)* is the delightful **Hotel Posada de San Francisco**, *Sandy's Choice*, (www.naftaconnect.com/hsanfrancisco, tel. 152-00-72, $95). Being next to the police station the hotel provides secure parking several blocks away. Unload the bike, then drive to the parking. The cab ride back is about $1. This classic colonial hotel has large rooms that include all amenities. It is suggested at you request an interior room overlooking the courtyard as the exterior ones can be noisy from all the activity on the street.

A ready smile is your reward whenever you travel in Mexico. (courtesy of MotoDiscovery)

There are many hotels in San Miguel in all price ranges. Stop by the tourist information center located next to the police station at El Jardin for current availabilities and prices.

San Miguel de Allende, pop. 80,000, is a crown jewel of Mexican national monument cities and a favorite of Americans, many who retire here. Even more have homes they use for only part of the year. San Miguel has several arts and crafts schools that attract international students of all persuasions. It also is known for its Spanish language schools and many people come to stay a month to learn the language, although the multicultural flavor of San Miguel makes knowing Spanish unnecessary. Of the many languages being spoken here, very few will be Spanish. The protected colonial architecture, monuments, fountains, churches, as well as the mix of people make San Miguel a delight.

San Miguel was founded in 1542 by a Franciscan friar, **Fray Juan de San Miguel**, as an outpost to bring the Christian religion to the "pagan" Indians. By 1555 the road connecting with Mexico City was completed and a fort was established to protect the silver shipments coming from other areas. It was the home of **Ignacio Allende** during early 1800s, the time of the Mexican revolution. Although Allende was captured and killed by the Spanish in 1811 (after the first attempt for freedom from the Spanish), it was a full ten years before the revolution was finally successful. In 1826 the town was renamed in his honor, and was designated a national monument city in 1926.

Life in San Miguel revolves around the central square, *El Jardin*, a most pleasant place to spend an hour or two in the evening watching all the activity. The town's major attraction is **La Parroquia,** the parish church. That the many steeples remind you of the Gothic churches of Europe is not just a coincidence. In the late 19th century after the church's first 200 years of existence, the facade was rebuilt by a local Indian, **Zeferino Gutiérrez,** who had no formal education. His only "plans" were picture postcards of European churches. Since these cards had only photographs of fronts of churches, the rear of this one maintains a style more typical of Mexico.

A visit to the **Museo Histórico de San Miguel de Allende,** located at Calle Cunda de Allende 1, has a fine overview of the history of this city and the surrounding area, as well as exhibits on Allende and the struggle for independence.

The *biblicteca pública* serves as a kind of clearing house for the expatriate community and provides copies of the local English language newspaper. A notice board advises of activities that might interest the visitor, apartments for rent, and other things. Taking a few minutes to read these notices will give you a true feeling of what it is like to live in this fine city as an American. You can also arrange a tour of some of the finer homes and gardens in the town here. San Miguel has many other pleasant plazas and a dazzling array of other churches to visit. Turn almost any corner and you will be in for another pleasant surprise. If you are interested in art, there are several galleries. Shopping for art, handicrafts, jewelry, and other fine items is a major activity for many visitors to San Miguel.

Day 4 San Miguel to Guanajuato and Return

Distance *125 miles (200 km) round trip*
Features *A day trip to the colonial city of Guanajuato has many sights worth a visit and quite a bit of history, too. After you leave Dolores Hidalgo the road climbs and twists until you have delightful views of the broad plain below. This is quite an altitude change so don't base your gear requirements on the temperature in San Miguel. As you approach Guanajuato you will find fantastic views of the town below you.*

Now how will I get this home? Ceramics are a specialty of Dolores Hidalgo.

From the *El Jardin* head south on the one way street going downhill (Cuna de Allende) and you will soon come to a T-intersection where the signs to Dolores Hidalgo are clearly marked to the left. Follow these signs out of the city. After 24 miles (40 km) follow the signs toward Guanajuato. To visit the town of Dolores Hidalgo follow the centro signs. To head directly to Guanajuato take the four-lane divided street that bypasses most of Dolores Hidalgo.

The national monument town of **Dolores Hidalgo** is known as the "Cradle of National Independence." At midnight on September 15, 1810, **Father Miguel Hidalgo y Costilla** called his parishioners to the local church by ringing the bell. He then made the adored *Grito de Dolores* speech declaring Mexican independence. Today the 16th of September is still celebrated as Independence Day and politicians throughout Mexico repeat an altered version of the *grito*. The church bell is rung on this day only each year. The home of Father Hidalgo, **Casa de Don Miguel Hidalgo**, at Morelos #1 is now a museum containing items relating to his life and times. His statue is in the main square.

Dolores Hidalgo is a pleasant town with a wonderful central plaza. It is noted for its hand glazed ceramics and the streets are lined with various stores selling colorful jugs, plates, tiles, and anything else that can be created in ceramic. Factor in an hour or two to explore this town.

Father Miguel Hidalgo y Costilla

Popularly known as the "Father of Mexican Independence," Father Miguel Hidalgo y Costilla was quite an unusual person. Born in 1753, he attended college and was ordained as a priest. Although he later taught college and became a rector, some of his views and ways led to a visit with the Inquisition in 1800. It is said that he questioned some of the basic beliefs of the Catholic Church, such as the virgin birth and the infallibility of the pope. It is also said that he gambled and had a mistress. Hidalgo escaped the Inquisition but was sent to the small town of Dolores in 1804 to be the local priest.

Hidalgo became involved with the move for independence when he met Ignacio Allende, and in 1810 he issued his now famous call for independence, the *Grito de Dolores*. At this point he became a true revolutionary and led troops as they attempted to free Mexico from Spanish dominance. As a result of this and his continuing public speeches against the church, he was excommunicated on October 13, 1810. As the Spanish gradually gained ground against the Mexicans, Miguel Hidalgo was captured and shot by a firing squad on July 30, 1811.

In a final, bizarre twist in this man's history, Hidalgo's head, along with three others, Allende's included, were returned to Guanajuato and hung from a public building near the main square, where they remained for almost ten years. This backfired on the Spanish in that rather than intimidate the Mexicans, it became a battle cry. The hooks that held the heads are still on the building today.   ✪

Beyond Dolores Hidalgo the road to Guanajuato twists and turns for 36 miles (60 km) of great motorcycling.

As you approach Guanajuato, one of the most famous churches in Mexico, officially known as **La Iglesia de San Cayetano,** but commonly called **La Valenciana,** will be on your left about halfway down the hill; it is well worth a visit. A view of the Valenciana mine is available from the parking lot on the right side of the road next to the church. This is the most prolific of Mexican silver mines, at one time producing almost 25 percent of the world's silver; it's still in operation today. When the daughter of the mine's owner got married in the nearby church, he had the path from his house lain with silver ingots.

Guanajuato is a large metropolitan city that can have serious traffic problems. I suggest you park your bike at a hotel with secure parking and

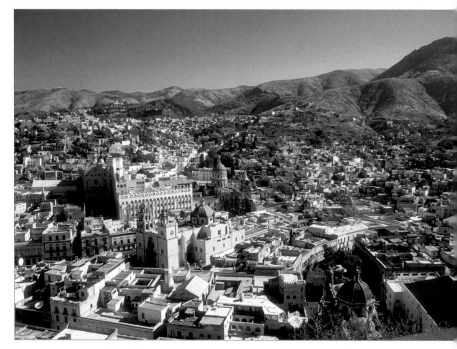

Guanajuato, a city of churches, rests in a deep valley. (courtesy of MotoDiscovery)

explore the city on foot. By following the signs toward Leon or Silao, you will find the hotel **Hacienda de las Cobos** on your left, at Padre Hidalgo #3 and Ave. Juarez #153 (tel. 473-732-03-50 or 732-92-70, $75). It has secure parking in a courtyard and a back door off the patio so you can walk to the sights in and around the central plaza. Should you wish to stay overnight in Guanajuato (which I highly recommend), this is a more than adequate hotel.

Since the city sits in a high valley surrounded by mountains, the streets are not laid out in a grid pattern and it can be quite confusing to navigate. It is best explored by foot. Many of the streets run underground, built inside old mineshafts and river courses. You can hire a taxi to take you on a short tour.

With a population of approximately 120,000, **Guanajuato** was once the home of some of the richest people in the world. The vast lodes of silver and gold located near Guanajuato led to the building of some magnificent mansions which are still in existence today. At one time almost a third of the world's silver was mined in the area. Guanajuato also played a crucial role in the **Mexican War of Independence,** and there are many good museums

Future bikers.

documenting this period. Today, Guanajuato is a vibrant, bustling city with a university whose more than 15,000 students add a spirit of youth to this historic colonial city. The city is also known for music: bands play, strolling groups fill the plazas, and young men, called *estudiantinas,* wander the streets until all hours of the night playing to all who are willing to listen (and a few who are not).

With the discovery of the **La Valenciana mine** in 1558, the city rapidly grew in population and wealth. At the start of the War of Independence, it was one of the most prosperous cities in all of New Spain. Although it was the third city to be captured by the rebels in 1810, it was the first of any size. It was quickly retaken by the Spanish, however, who punished the population by holding a "lottery of death" where the winners were killed.

With so many sights to see in Guanajuato, plan an overnight stay, if at all possible. The **Alhondiga de Granaditas,** originally a granary and later a jail and fortress, now contains an excellent museum. When the rebels first attempted to take Guanajuato, the Spanish and their supporters fled to this building and locked themselves in. On September 28, 1810, a young rebel named **Jose de los Reyes Martinez** managed to set the gates ablaze before being killed by gunfire, thus allowing the rebels to enter and overcome the

Spanish. This young Indian, known as **El Pipila**, became a national hero and a statue of him with his torch sits on top of a hill in the center of the city. For ten years after the Spanish retook Guanajuato, the severed heads of Hidalgo, Allende, Jimenez, and Aldama hung in metal cages from the corners of the roof of this building. The hooks are still here. The building now houses an excellent history museum as well as an art gallery. Colorful and graphic murals by **Chavez Morado** line the stairwells.

The **Jardin de la Union** is the center of the action in Guanajuato. In the evenings, nearby university students gather on the tree-shaded grounds to socialize and watch the ever-changing scene. The **Teatro Juarez**, built from 1873 to 1903, is located on the Jardin de la Union. The interior decor is definitely French and it reflects the wealth of the people of Guanajuato during the time of its construction. Not for the faint of heart or the weak of stomach, the very unusual **Museo de las Momias** (Mummy Museum) contains the remains of bodies that were preserved after burial due to the climate and soil conditions. It contains more than a hundred mummies of all types, including babies and pregnant women. Located at Calz. del Panteon, the museum is best visited by taxi.

Shiny shoes are very important to Mexican men. It will cost you about a dollar to get your motorcycle boots shined.

Day 5 San Miguel de Allende to Tamazunchale

Distance   *235 miles (380 km)*
Features   *This day starts out in the high desert on high speed multi-lane highways and ends up with wonderful twisting and turning roads through jungle. You will start out cool and dry and end up in hot and wet humid conditions; along the way you will descend almost 6,000 feet in elevation.*

Churches are around every corner in San Miguel de Allende.

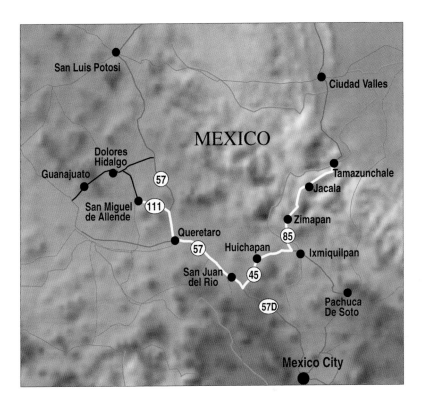

From El Jardin head south as you did going to Guanajuato on Cuna de Allende and after two blocks make a turn right. This is the first right turn opportunity. At the T-intersection, turn left and follow the cobblestone street as it winds the way up the hill. A wonderful overlook with ample parking will soon be quite evident. After this stop and the mandatory picture taking, continue up the hill to the PEMEX and, of all things, a "world class" shopping center. This series of high-end stores gives you a good indication of the number of rich gringos and gringas that maintain homes in San Miguel.

Go straight and in a very short time the left turn onto Hwy. 111 to **San Luis Potosi** is clearly marked. In 21 miles (34 km) you will reach the intersection with Hwy. 57. This can be confusing as you must take the overpass over the large four lane road, do a U-turn, and then enter the highway. Follow the signs to Querétaro/Mexico. Stay on this multilane toll highway for the next 37 miles (60 km) bypassing **Queretaro** and continuing in the direction of Mexico (Mexico City) now on Hwy. 57D. After passing through the towns of **San Juan del Rio** and **Paso de Mata**, watch for the turn to **Huichapan**. Head east on Hwy. 45 for 60 miles (100 km) to the

Laundry is done a little differently in Mexico.

intersection with Hwy. 85 in **Ixmiquilpan** where you will turn left (north) toward Zimapan/Tamazunchale/Cuidad Valles. After 115 miles (185 km) of some magnificent motorcycle riding, you will arrive in your home for the evening. Do not be fooled by the mileage today or the progress you will make early on! The last portion of riding, while wonderful, will be slow. The 90 miles from **Jacala** to **Tamazunchale** with its magnificent descent into the jungles once took me more than three hours of pretty hard riding!

The choice of overnight lodging in Tamazunchale is limited. The **Hotel Tamazunchale** ($35), located on your right in the middle of town, is a more than adequate place with hot water and flush toilets. Parking is right next door and a guard will look over your steed throughout the night. A few other options are available, but all are a level or two below this one.

Mountainous back roads with unbelievable scenery will have you stopping often.

Day 6 Tamazunchale to Santa Engracia

Distance *190 miles (300 km)*
Features *This day starts with more twisting through the jungle on the old highway and gradually gives way to the more "civilized" open roads through tropical flatlands. An easy day with a delightful overnight destination.*

Throughout Mexico, roadside shrines mark spots where "souls have left this earth." Ride carefully, so there won't be a shrine with your name on it!

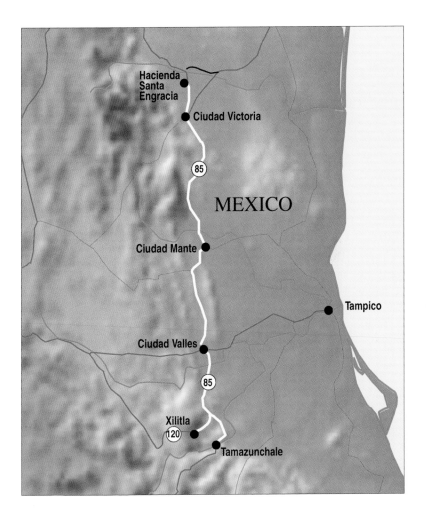

Continue north on the old Pan American Highway (Hwy. 85) for 50 miles (80 km) to **Ciudad Valles** and continue straight through town. As you ride toward **Cuidad Mante** the road is bordered by low savannah lands. Keep going on Hwy. 85, toward **Cuidad Victoria,** where you want to follow the signs to **Monterrey** to bypass downtown. About 22 miles (35 km) after leaving Victoria the left turn to **Santa Engracia** is clearly marked. From here it is 12 miles (20 km) to the hacienda through citrus groves and several small villages, just keep following the pavement. As you approach the village of Santa Engracia the white building on the right with large palm trees is your destination. If you reach the end of the pavement you will have gone too far.

Hacienda Santa Engracia (tel. 131-6-10-61, $55) is an absolute must overnight stay. The family has owned the land since the 1500s when it was given to them by Spanish land grant. Once the family home, the Hacienda provides a real feel for colonial Mexico. The accommodations are basic, but modern with all amenities. The grounds are lush and peaceful with a nice pool area and even a tennis court. No need to read the menu here—you'll eat what the family is having! With only 26 rooms, the Hacienda can quickly fill up on weekends; during the week you may well be the only guests. This is a treat not to be missed and a wonderful way to spend your last night in Mexico.

Edwin James' surreal dream lies decaying in the midst of the jungle near Xilitla.

Side trip

About 22 miles (35 km) North of Tamazunchale, Hwy. 120, toward **Xilitla** is clearly marked. Take this left turn and travel 8 miles (12 km) to visit one of the strangest sites I have ever seen. As you approach the town, take a right turn on a dirt road. (If you cross the bridge you have gone too far.) The ride down the dirt is not far and it was in good condition the last time I was there. Your destination is **Las Pozas** (the pools) and **La Casa de Inglés** (English house), the "home" of the late eccentric millionaire Edward James, friend of artists Dali and Picasso. His love for their style of art will soon be evident! Rumored to be the illegitimate son of King Edward VII, James escaped to this remote area and spent more than twenty years building surrealist concrete structures and planning a vast estate, most of which is unfinished and now being overtaken by the jungle. The river that runs through this area has several pools that are popular swimming holes for the local children. Local vendors will have their wares spread on blankets for your viewing. Walk the grounds, enjoy the jungle, and try to imagine what was going on in this man's mind. After your visit (plan on at least an hour) return to the highway and continue north.

Day 7   Santa Engracia to Pharr, Texas

Distance   *155 miles (250 km)*

Features   *The goal today is to arrive back in the United States safely. The ride is on two-lane roads ending at the rather small border crossing at Pharr/ Reynosa. You will have time to make this crossing and continue, at your pleasure, on into the U.S. By the way, don't fall prey to "border fever." Slow down, be patient, and soon you will be telling tales of your adventures in Mexico (some of them even true!).*

Retrace the route from Santa Engracia to Hwy. 85. Turn right and go 4 miles (7 km) south and take the clearly-marked left turn. After another 7 miles (12 km) you will reach a T-intersection with no signage. Turn left (north) onto Hwy.101. From here just follow the signs to **Reynosa** (there is a left turn onto highway 97 after about 50 miles). Upon entering Reynosa follow the signs to the international bridge. Be sure and check out with Mexican authorities before crossing the bridge!

Most Mexican towns are built around a central plaza.

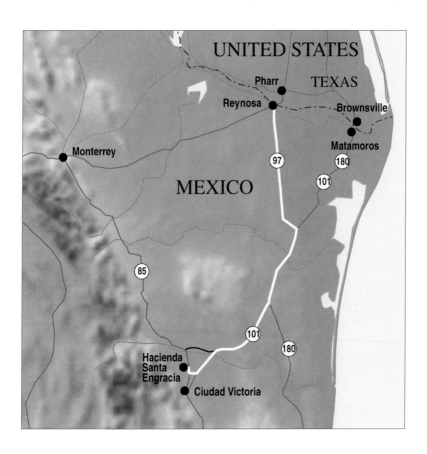

Index

Motorcycle Services

MOTORCYCLE TRANSPORT

If you have limited time available and live far from Texas, consider shipping your motorcycle to your starting city and flying down to pick it up. This will maximize your riding time.

The cost for this service varies greatly depending on several factors. Check out the websites shown below for more information and to get a quick quote. These companies all use special motorcycle-appropriate skids with pads and tie-downs (no crating necessary); all are designed to deliver your bike without damage. You will be amazed at how easy and efficient they make this process.

Federal/Allied Transport (Rhonda Nagel)
101 National Road
East Peoria, Illinois. 61611
800-747-4100, ext 222
www.funtransport.com

Federal ships more than 1,000 motorcycles per month and also handled all of the motorcycles for the traveling Guggenheim exhibit, so they have plenty of experience. Your bike will be handled by a special division within Allied Van Lines and will not be shipped with household goods.

J.C. Motors/Specialized Motorcycle Transport
16591 Noyes Ave.
Irvine, CA 92626
800-730-3151
www.motorcycleshipping.com

Part of a large motorcycle parts supplier and one of the larger California dealers, this company touts itself as one of us and the "experts" in the field shipping over 700 motorcycles a month. Their rates are very competitive.

Daily Direct LLC – Haul Bikes
4600 North 124th St.
Milwaukee, WI. 53225
1-800-haulbikes
www.haulbikes.com
These people ship over 1,000 bikes per month and advertise that all drivers are bike owners themselves.

MOTORCYCLE RENTALS

If you live far from Texas or have limited time, it might make sense just to rent a bike for your adventure. While you lose the familiarity with your own machine and its associated attachments, you gain the opportunity to try out a different bike without making a purchase.

If you do an internet search for motorcycle rentals in Texas, you will find several pages of offerings from Harleys to Ducatis and everything in between. Check these companies out carefully; ask for references from past customers, etc. In other words, "buyer beware!"

From our research it would appear that there are a few reputable companies renting bikes in Texas. Harley's seem to be the easiest bikes to rent associated with local dealers. We would suggest you check out the websites www.eagleriders.com or www.streeteagle.com to determine if there are locations that fit your needs. Sport bike and other brand riders should try www.sportryderrentals.com.

Please note that this is not an endorsement or advertisement for any of these companies, but they do seem legitimate in our research efforts and are usually associated with a dealership or manufacturer. Several companies operate under a holding company umbrella (read liability laws) called MBA holdings and, again, these appear to be good folks trying to provide a service to us in need.

There is no reason that with just a little work you can't find that bike you need to ride available for rent in Texas.

MOTORCYCLE DEALERSHIPS

Motorcycle Dealerships are numerous in all the major cities in Texas and with few exceptions will be readily available in most small towns through which you will be riding. This does not hold true for the West Texas ride as it goes through some very remote areas. The following dealers, all of which were very helpful in preparation of this book, are located in our hub cities and are recommended. Usually they are located near the airport and are willing to help you in any way they can, including accepting your bike from a freight company. It is suggested that you leave any last minute maintenance to their good hands. Please support these dealers with a purchase or two during your visit. If you have a bike of another make, they can direct you to that local dealership.

San Antonio
Alamo City Harley-Davidson
1105 IH 35 N., San Antonio, TX. 78233, 210-646-0499

Joe Harrison Motor Sports
9710 IH 35 N., San Antonio, TX. 78233, 210-656-9400, 800-859-5698
Honda, Suzuki, and Triumph

Houston
Stubbs Cycles
4436 Telephone Rd., Houston, TX, 713-644-7535
Honda, Suzuki, Harley-Davidson, and Buell

Houston Motor Sports
11941 Southwest Freeway, Houston, TX, 281-530-8600
BMW

Houston Kawasaki
3530 Bering Dr., Houston, TX. 77057, 713-783-3844

El Paso
Barnet Harley-Davidson/Buell
8272 Gateway East, El Paso, TX, 800-736-8173 or 915-592-5804
www.barnettharley.com
   This dealership advertises as the "world's largest Harley-Davidson dealer" and a visit will have you believing it. The new store is worth the trip just to roam around and gawk.

Mr. Honda
6020 Gateway E., El Paso, TX. 79905, 915-545-2453
Honda, Yamaha, Suzuki, Triumph, KTM, Moto Guzzi, and Ducati

A Little Spanish

You can travel in northern Mexico and speak no Spanish, but I don't recommend it since it will make things more difficult and cause frustration. Please spend a few hours with some tapes to pick up a few basic phrases. Not only will this help you directly in your travels, you will likely be rewarded with a friendly smile and assistance for having made an attempt to communicate. Since Spanish pronunciation is very regular, a little time spent familiarizing yourself with the rules can reap big rewards.

PRONUNCIATION

Most letters in Spanish are pronounced very similar to their English counterparts. These few simple rules note some of the general variations. You can practice by applying this guide to other words listed here.

Spanish Letter	English Sound	Example	Pronounced
A	ah (yacht)	*padre*	PAH-dray
E	ay (day)	*español*	ays-pah-NYOHL
I	ee (meet)	*libro*	LEE-broh
O	oh (open)	*moto*	MOH-toh
U	oo (tooth)	*mucho*	MOO-choh
AU	ow (cow)	*auto*	OW-toh
AI	y (type)	*baile*	BYE-lay
IE	yeh (yet)	*abierto*	ah-VYER-toh
UE	weh (wet)	*bueno*	BWEH-noh
C (before a, o, u)	k (cat)	*campo*	KAHM-poh
C (before e, i)	s (cent)	*cinco*	SEEN-koh
G (before a, o, u)	g (go)	*guerra*	GAY-rrah
G (before e, i)	h (hot)	*general*	hay-nay-RAHL
H	silent	*hasta*	AHS-tah
J	h (hot)	*jardín*	hahr-DEEN
LL	y (yes)	*pollo*	POH-yoh
Ñ	ny (canyon)	*señorita*	say-nyohr-REE-tah
QU	k (keep)	*que*	kay
R	roll once	*caro*	KAH-doh
RR	roll twice	*perro*	PAY-rroh
S	s (see)	*rosa*	ROH-sah
V	b (book)	*primavera*	pree-mah-BAY-rah
X	s (sign)	*examinar*	ays-ahm-mee-NAHR
Z	s (sane)	*zapato*	sah-PAH-toh

STRESS AND ACCENTS

Spanish also uses very regular rules to apply stress to syllables in a word:

Words ending in a vowel, N, or S are stressed on the second-to-last syllable.

Words ending in a consonant other than N or S are stressed on the last syllable.

Words that are exceptions to the two rules above must have an accent mark over the stressed syllable.

DAILY POLITENESS

Listed below is a basic vocabulary of words and phrases which you can use to practice your pronunciation; consult a good Spanish-English dictionary for less common words. The first two words on the list are the most important.

thank you	gracias	GRAH-syahs
please	por favor	POR fah-VOHR
you're welcome	de nada	DAY NAH-dah
good morning	buenos días	BWAY-nos DEE-ahs
good afternoon	buenas tardes	BWAY-nahs TAHR-days
good night	buenas noches	BWAY-nahs NOH-chays
How are you?	¿Cómo está?	COH-moh ays-TAH
I am fine	Estoy bien	ays-TOY BYEHN
excuse me	perdóneme.	pehr-DOH-nay-may
Goodbye!	¡Adiós!	ah-DYOHS
yes	sí	SEE
no	no	NOH
bad	malo	MAH-loh
good	bueno	BWAY-noh
more	más	MAHS
less	menos	MAY-nohs

AT THE BORDER

bike title	título de propiedad	TEE-too-loh DAY proh-pree-ay-DAD
registration	registración	ray-hee-strah-SYOHN
Customs	Aduana	ah-DWAH-nah
Immigration	Immigración	eem-ee-grah-SYOHN
identification	identificación	ee-dayn-tee-fee-cah-SYOHN
passport	pasaporte	pah-sah-POHR-tay
tourist card	tarjeta de turista	tahr-HAY-tah day too-REE-stah
credit card	tarjeta de crédito	tahr-HAY-tah day CRAY-dee-toh
vehicle permit	permiso de importación	pehr-MEE-soh DAY eem-pohr-tah-SYOHN
	temporal de vehículo	tehm-pohr-AHL DAY bay-HEE-kyoo-loh

BASIC VERBS AND QUESTIONS

I want . . .	*Quiero . . .*	KYAY-doh
I need . . .	*Necesito . . .*	nay-say-SEE-toh
I have . . .	*Tengo . . .*	TEHN-goh
Do you have . . . ?	*¿Tiene . . . ?*	TYAY-nay
Do you speak English?	*¿Hablan inglés?*	AH-blan een-GLAYS
How much does this cost?	*¿Cuánto cuesta?*	KWAHN-toh KWAY-stah
I don't understand.	*No entiendo.*	NOH ayn-TYEHN-doh
Where is . . . ?	*¿Dónde está . . . ?*	DOHN-day ays-TAH
How far is . . . ?	*¿A qué distancia está . . . ?*	AH KAY dee-STAHN-syah ays-TAH
How long?	*¿Cuánto tiempo?*	KWAN-toh TYEM-poh

ON THE ROAD

left	*izquierda*	ees-KYEHR-dah
right	*derecha*	day-RRAY-chah
straight ahead	*derecho*	day-RRAY-choh
highway	*carretera*	kah-rray-TAY-dah
road	*camino*	cah-MEE-noh
street	*calle*	KAH-YAY
north	*norte*	NOHR-tay
south	*sur*	SOOD
east	*este*	AYS-tay
west	*oeste*	oh-AYS-tay
traffic light	*luz*	LOOS
blinking/flashing lights	*luces intermitentes*	LOO-says een-tehr-mee-TAYN-tays
gasoline	*gasolina*	gah-soh-LEE-nah
unleaded	*sin plomo, magna sin*	SEEN PLOH-mo, MAHG-nah SEEN
full	*lleno*	YAY-noh
oil	*aceite*	ah-say-EE-tay
puncture	*agujero*	ah-goo-HAY-doh
front tire/rim	*llanta delanteros*	YAHN-tah day-lan-TAY-dohs
back tire/rim	*llanta delantera trasera*	YAHN-tah day-lan-TAY-dah trah-SAY-dah
inner tube	*tubo interior*	TOO-boh een-tay-RYOHR
air/fuel filter	*filtro de aire/combustible*	FEEL-troh DAY AY-day/cohm-boo-STEE-blay
spark plugs	*bujías*	boo-HEE-ahs
gear box	*caja de cambio*	KAH-hah day KAHM-byoh
final drive	*transmisión*	trahns-mee-SYOHN
drive shaft	*eje transmisor*	AY-hay trans-mee-SOHR
chain	*cadena*	kah-DAY-nah
master link	*eslabón principal*	ays-lah-BOHN preen-see-PAHL

cooling system	*agua del radiador*	AH-gwah dehl rah-dee-ah-DOHR
anti-freeze	*anti-congelante*	AHN-tee cohn-gay-LAHN-tay
nut/bolt	*tornillo*	tohr-NEE-yoh
washer	*arandela*	ah-dahn-DAY-lah
compressed air	*aire a presión*	AY-day ah pray-SYOHN
axle	*eje*	AY-hay
front brakes	*frenos delanteros*	FRAY-nohs day-lan-TAY-dohs
rear brakes	*frenos traseros*	FRAY-nohs trah-SAY-dohs
brake/clutch fluid	*Liquido de freno/ embrague*	lee-KWEE-doh day FRAY-noh/aym-BRAH-gay
brake/clutch cable	*Cable de frenos/ embrague*	KAH-blay day FRAY-noh/aym-BRAH-gay
fuse	*fusible*	foo-SEE-blay
headlight bulb	*faro delantero*	FAH-doh day-lan-TAY-doh
taillight bulb	*bombilla piloto*	bohm-BEE-yah pee-LOH-toh
dead battery	*batería descargada*	bah-tay-REE-ah days-kahr-GAH-dah
distilled water	*agua destilada*	AH-gwah day-stee-LAH-dah
muffler	*mofle*	MOH-flay
spring	*muelle*	moo-AY-YAY

HIGHWAY SIGNS

These will generally give you no problem, as Mexico uses international symbols.

stop	*alto*	AHL-toh
keep to right	*conserve su derecha*	cohn-SEHR-bay soo day-RRAY-chah
dangerous curve	*curva peligrosa*	KOOHR-bah pay-lee-GROH-sah
no passing	*no rebase*	NOH ray-BAH-say
school zone	*zona escolar*	SOHN-ah ays-koh-LAHR
slow down	*disminuya su velocidad*	dees-mee-NOO-yah soo bay-loh-see-DAHD
danger	*peligro*	pay-LEE-groh
speed bumps	*topes/vibradores*	TOH-pays/bee-brah-DOHR-ays
toll route	*cuota*	KWOH-tah
free route	*libre*	LEE-bray
detour	*desviación*	des-vee-ah-SYOHN
men working	*hombres trabajando*	OHM-brays trah-bah-HAHN-doh
freeway	*autopista*	ow-toh-PEE-stah

ACCOMMODATIONS

hotel	*hotel*	oh-TEL
room	*habitación*	ah-vee-tah-SYOHN
for one person	*para una persona*	PAH-dah OO-nah pehr-SOH-nah
for two persons	*para dos personas*	PAH-dah DOHS pehr-SOH-nahs
one bed	*sencillo*	sen-SEE-yoh
two beds	*doble*	DOH-blay

with bath	con baño	cohn BAH-nyoh
hot water	agua caliente	AH-gwah kah-lee-AYN-tay
towel	toalla	toh-AH-yah
soap	jabón	ha-BOHN
toilet paper	papel higiénico	pah-PEHL ee-HYAY-nee-koh

NUMBERS

0	cero	SAY-doh
1	uno, una	OO-noh, OO-nah
2	dos	DOHS
3	tres	TRAYS
4	cuatro	KWAH-troh
5	cinco	SEEN-koh
6	seis	SAYS
7	siete	see-AY-tay
8	ocho	OH-choh
9	nueve	noo-AY-vay
10	diez	DYAYS
11	once	OHN-say
12	doce	DOH-say
13	trece	TRAY-say
14	catorce	kah-TOHR-say
15	quince	KEEN-say
16	dieciséis	dee-ay-see-SAYS
17	diecisiete	dee-ay-see-see-AY-tay
18	dieciocho	dee-ay-see-OH-cho
19	diecinueve	dee-ay-see-noo-AY-vay
20	veinte	BAYN-tay
21	veintiuno	bayn-tee-OO-noh
22	veintidós	bayn-tee-DOHS
30	treinta	TRAYN-tah
40	cuarenta	kwah-DAYN-tah
50	cincuenta	seen-KWAYN-tah
60	sesenta	say-SAYN-tah
70	setenta	say-TAYN-tah
80	ochenta	oh-CHAYN-tah
90	noventa	noh-BAYN-tah
100	cien	SYEN
200	doscientos	doh-SYEN-tohs
1000	mil	MEEL

ON THE MENU (LA CARTA)

TABLEWARE

spoon	*cuchara*	koo-CHAH-dah
knife	*cuchillo*	koo-CHEE-yoh
plate	*plato*	PLAH-toh
fork	*tenedor*	tay-nay-DOHR
cup	*taza*	TAH-sah
glass	*vaso*	BAH-soh
napkin	*servilleta*	sehr-bee-YAY-tah

DRINKS *(BEBIDAS)*

water	*agua*	AH-gwah
mineral water	*agua mineral*	AH-gwah mee-nehr-AHL
coffee	*café*	kah-FAY
coffee with hot milk	*café con leche*	kah-FAY kohn LAY-chay
coffee with cream	*café con crema*	kah-FAY kohn KRAY-mah
black coffee	*café negro*	kah-FAY NAY-groh
soft drinks	*refrescos*	ray-FRAYS-kohs
fruit juice	*jugo*	HOO-goh
tea	*té*	TAY
beer	*cerveza*	sehr-BAY-sah
red wine	*vino rojo*	BEE-noh RROH-hoh
white wine	*vino blanco*	BEE-noh BLAHN-koh

BREAKFAST *(DESAYUNO)*

bread	*pan*	PAHN
toast	*pan tostado*	PAHN tohs-TAH-doh
butter	*mantequilla*	man-tay-KEE-yah
jelly	*mermelada*	mehr-may-LAH-dah
eggs	*huevos*	hoo-AY-vohs
scrambled eggs	*huevos revueltos*	hoo-AY-vohs ray-VWAYL-tohs
fried/sunny-side up eggs	*huevos fritos*	hoo-AY-vohs FREE-tohs
eggs scrambled with chiles, onions, and tomatoes	*huevos mexicanos*	hoo-AY-vohs may-hee-KAHN-ohs
fried eggs covered with salsa	*huevos rancheros*	hoo-AY-vohs rrahn-CHAY-dos
sweet rolls	*pan dulce*	pahn DOOL-say
bacon	*tocino*	toh-SEE-noh
ham	*jamón*	hah-MOHN

MEATS AND POULTRY

chicken	*pollo*	POH-yoh
chicken breast	*pechuga*	pay-CHOO-gah
turkey	*pavo*	PAH-boh
duck	*pato*	PAH-toh
meat	*carne*	KAHR-nay

beef	*res*	RAYS
beefsteak	*bistec*	BEES-tayk
hamburger	*hamburguesa*	ahm-boor-GAY-sah
pork	*puerco*	PWEHR-koh
pork sausage (hot)	*chorizo*	choh-DEE-soh
pork rinds	*chicharrón*	chee-chah-RROHN
goat	*cabra*	KAH-brah
young goat	*cabrito*	kah-BREE-toh
veal	*ternera*	tay-NAY-dah

SEAFOOD

fish	*pescado*	pays-KAH-doh
filet	*filete de pescado*	fee-LAY-tay day pays-KAH-doh
fried whole fish	*frito pescado*	FREE-toh pays-KAH-doh
fried filet of fish	*filete de pescado frito*	fee-LAY-tay day pays-KAH-doh FREE-toh
tuna	*atún*	ah-TOON
bass	*corvina*	kohr-BEE-nah
red snapper	*huachinango*	wah-chee-NAHN-goh
salmon	*salmón*	sal-MOHN
shark	*tiburón*	tee-boo-DOHN
trout	*trucha*	TROO-chah
lobster	*langosta*	lahn-GOH-stah
snail	*caracol*	kah-dah-COHL
clams	*almejas*	ahl-MAY-hahs
squid	*calamar*	kah-lah-MAHR
shrimp	*camarones*	kah-mah-RROH-nays

FRUITS

orange	*naranja*	nah-DAHN-hah
apple	*manzana*	mahn-SAHN-ah
lime	*limón*	lee-MOHN
mango	*mango*	MAHN-goh
grape	*uva*	OO-bah
grapefruit	*toronja*	toh-DOHN-hah

PREPARATION

grilled over charcoal	*al carbón*	ahl kahr-BOHN
grilled	*asada*	ah-SAH-dah
boiled	*cocido*	koh-SEE-doh
breaded, Italian-style	*milanesa*	mee-lah-NAY-sah
fried	*frito*	FREE-toh
rare	*poco cocido*	POH-koh koh-SEE-doh
well done	*bien cocido*	BYEHN koh-SEE-doh
smoked	*ahumado*	ah-oo-MAH-doh
baked	*al horno*	ahl OHR-noh
fried in butter and garlic	*al mojo de ajo*	ahl MOH-hoh day AH-hoh

broiled or baked and covered in   *veracruz*   bay-dah-KROOS
a tomato sauce with olives

VEGETABLES

tomato	*tomate*	toh-MAH-tay
onion	*cebolla*	say-BOH-lah
mushrooms	*champiñones*	chahm-pee-NYOH-nays
carrot	*zanahoria*	sah-nah-oh-DEE-ah
radish	*rábano*	RRAH-bah-noh
potatoes	*papas*	PAH-pahs
beans	*frijoles*	free-HOH-lays
asparagus	*espàrragos*	ays-PAH-rrah-gos
avocado	*aquacate*	ah-kwah-KAH-tay
lettuce	*lechuga*	lay-CHOO-gah
garlic	*ajo*	AH-hoh

MEXICAN SPECIALTIES

tortilla presented with almost every meal, these can be made thick or thin, from corn, wheat, or flour

enchilada combinations of meat, chicken, or seafood with beans, cheese, salsa, or chili, rolled in a *tortilla,* then baked

burrito same as an *enchilada* but wrapped in a wheat or flour *tortilla*

torta sandwich on a roll

taco same as an *enchilada* or *burrito,* but wrapped in a soft corn *tortilla*

chiles rellenos deep-fried chilies stuffed with cheese

guacamole mashed avocado mixed with onion, tomato, chili, and lemon, served cold

quesadilla a flour *tortilla* topped with cheese, then baked

tamal corn dough stuffed with combinations of meat, cheeses, and beans, wrapped and steamed in corn husks

sincronizada grilled ham and cheese sandwich

SWEETS

ice cream	*helado*	ay-LAH-doh
cream caramel	*flan*	FLAHN
crepe	*crepa*	KRAY-pah
pastry	*pastel*	pahs-TAYL

Additional Resources

There is no shortage of other reference materials regarding travel in Texas. Not so much on motorcycling though. Carry this book in your tankbag as a complete guide to your rides. If you are a true history buff, however, and want to better understand what made Texas what it is today, I suggest you read *Texas* by James Michener; even though it's fiction, it is based on historical fact and can be very enlightening.

Most maps of Texas will be of little use to you, especially for the Hill Country and east Texas rides, because regular road maps can't cover such big areas in the necessary detail. Try the *Texas Atlas & Gazetteer* by Delorme for a closer look at roads and possible alternate rides (available from Whitehorse Press; www.whitehorsepress.com).

An excellent magazine that can help familiarize you with the Lone Star State is *Texas Highways,* published monthly by the Texas Department of Tourism (800-839-4997; www.texashighways.com).

The Texas Department of Tourism does a very good job of promoting the state and will flood you with information, if you contact them (800-452-9292; either www.dot.state.tx.us or www.traveltex.com).

About the Authors

Neal and Sandy Davis are long-time world travelers and adventurers having worked and lived for extended periods of time in seven different countries spanning four continents. They have lost count of the number of countries they have visited as tourists only. Many of these travels and adventures have been via motorcycle.

Neal and Sandy currently "home base" on a ranch near Glacier Park in Montana ("the Ponderosa"), where they spend their spare time enjoying that wonderful part of the world and planning their next expedition.

After retiring from a successful career in the oil industry, Neal served in various capacities with organized motorcycle tour operators in Europe and Mexico. Neal's previous books include *Motorcycle Journeys Through Northern Mexico, Motorcycle Journeys Through Southern Mexico* and *Motorcycle Journeys Through Texas*.

Sandy, during her checkered career, has worked as a welder on nuclear power plants and refineries, obtained degrees in both Engineering and Nursing along the way and has been in charge of the medical care for expat employees on large construction projects in remote locations throughout the world. Sandy collaborated on this project to update two of the books mentioned above and to add a "feminine viewpoint" to the narrative.

Neal considers himself a Texan and Sandy, while having lived there on three separate occasions, still considers herself just a simple Montana ranch matron (think Barbara Stanwick in *The Big Valley*).

Neal and Sandy are currently serving a two-year mission with The Church of Jesus Christ of Latter-Day Saints in the Democratic Republic of Congo where they are working to help others who are in need and less fortunate.